# Conference on Empirical Methods in Natural Language Processing (EMNLP 2021)



Tutorial Abstracts

Punta Cana, Dominican Republic and Online
7-11 November 2021

ISBN: 978-1-7138-9163-5

**Printed from e-media with permission by:**

Curran Associates, Inc.
57 Morehouse Lane
Red Hook, NY 12571

**Some format issues inherent in the e-media version may also appear in this print version.**



Association for Computational Linguistics
209 N. Eighth Street
Stroudsburg, Pennsylvania 18360

Phone: 1-570-476-8006
Fax: 1-570-476-0860

acl@aclweb.org

**Additional copies of this publication are available from:**

Curran Associates, Inc.
57 Morehouse Lane
Red Hook, NY 12571 USA
Phone: 845-758-0400
Fax: 845-758-2633
Email: curran@proceedings.com
Web: www.proceedings.com

EMNLP 2021

# The 2021 Conference on Empirical Methods in Natural Language Processing

## Tutorial Abstracts

November 10 - 11, 2021

# Introduction

Tutorials offer a great opportunity for the EMNLP conference attendees (both virtually and on-site), to be introduced with or get up to speed with various research topics. They are lectured by people doing cutting-edge research in those areas and often serve as very concise and useful summaries of previous and ongoing research, also outlining challenges and future perspectives.

As in previous years, tutorials were selected by a unified review process: this year it spanned four conferences (EACL, NAACL-HLT, ACL-IJCNLP, and EMNLP). We received a total of 35 submissions, and six tutorial proposals or extremely high-quality were selected for presentation at EMNLP 2021. The tutorials cover a range of diverse topics as follows: crowdsourcing and data collection (T1), financial opinion mining (T2), knowledge-enriched natural language generation (T3), multi-domain multilingual QA (T4), robustness and adversarial examples in NLP (T5), and syntax in end-to-end NLP models (T6). We are pleased to see that our tutorial presenters are experts all around the world, and some tutorials include trans-national and even trans-continental collaborations.

We would like to thank the 2021 tutorial co-chairs of EACL, NAACL-HLT and ACL-IJCNLP for their work on tutorial selection, the EMNLP 2021 publication chairs Greg Durrett, Loic Barrault and Yansong Feng for their help with preparing the proceedings, the general chair Marie-Francine Moens for coordinating everything so smoothly, the program co-chairs Xuanjing Huang, Lucia Specia, and Scott Wen-tau Yih, the website chair Miryam de Lhoneux, the handbook chair Els Lefever, as well as the virtual infrastructure chairs Zhaopeng Tu, Dani Yogatama, and Quynh Do. We also extend our thanks to all student volunteers and all the other people not named here who helped us one way or another during the long months of selection and preparation. Finally, one big thankyou goes to the tutorial authors for submitting their tutorial proposals and preparing their tutorial materials, and for their flexibility and collaboration in these exceptional times of virtual and hybrid conferences.

Following the spirit of the whole EMNLP 2021 conference, the tutorial presentations will be a mixture of online, on-site and hybrid presentations. We hope you'll enjoy the tutorial program at EMNLP 2021!

EMNLP 2021 Tutorial Co-chairs
Jing Jiang
Ivan Vulić

**General Chair:**

Marie-Francine Moens, *KU Leuven*

**Program Chairs:**

Xuanjing Huang, *Fudan University*
Lucia Specia, *Imperial College London*
Scott Wen-tau Yih, *Facebook AI Research*

**Tutorial Chairs:**

Jing Jiang, *Singapore Management University*
Ivan Vulić, *University of Cambridge and PolyAI*

## Table of Contents

# Conference Program

**November 10, 2021, 9:00-12:30 (UTC-4)**

*Crowdsourcing Beyond Annotation: Case Studies in Benchmark Data Collection*
Alane Suhr, Clara Vania, Nikita Nangia, Maarten Sap, Mark Yatskar, Samuel R. Bowman and Yoav Artzi

*Financial Opinion Mining*
Chung-Chi Chen, Hen-Hsen Huang and Hsin-Hsi Chen

*Knowledge-Enriched Natural Language Generation*
Wenhao Yu, Meng Jiang, Zhiting Hu, Qingyun Wang, Heng Ji and Nazneen Rajani

**November 11, 2021, 9:00-12:30 (UTC-4)**

*Multi-Domain Multilingual Question Answering*
Sebastian Ruder and Avi Sil

*Robustness and Adversarial Examples in Natural Language Processing*
Kai-Wei Chang, He He, Robin Jia and Sameer Singh

*Syntax in End-to-End Natural Language Processing*
Hai Zhao, Rui Wang and Kehai Chen

# Crowdsourcing Beyond Annotation: Case Studies in Benchmark Data Collection

**Alane Suhr**[1], **Clara Vania**[2], **Nikita Nangia**[3], **Maarten Sap**[4]
**Mark Yatskar**[5], **Samuel R. Bowman**[3] and **Yoav Artzi**[1]

[1]Cornell University [2]Amazon [3]New York University
[4]University of Washington [5]University of Pennsylvania

{suhr, yoav}@cs.cornell.edu
{nikitanangia, bowman}@nyu.edu vaniclar@amazon.co.uk
msap@cs.washington.edu myatskar@seas.upenn.edu

**Abstract**

Crowdsourcing from non-experts is one of the most common approaches to collecting data and annotations in NLP. Even though it is such a fundamental tool in NLP, crowdsourcing use is largely guided by common practices and the personal experience of researchers. Developing a theory of crowdsourcing use for practical language problems remains an open challenge. However, there are various principles and practices that have proven effective in generating high quality and diverse data. This tutorial exposes NLP researchers to such data collection crowdsourcing methods and principles through a detailed discussion of a diverse set of case studies.

## 1 Tutorial Description

Crowdsourcing from non-experts is one of the most common approaches to collecting data and annotations in NLP. It has been applied to a plethora of tasks, including question answering (Rajpurkar et al., 2016; Choi et al., 2018), textual entailment (Williams et al., 2018; Khot et al., 2018), instruction following (Bisk et al., 2016; Misra et al., 2018; Suhr et al., 2019a; Chen et al., 2019a), visual reasoning (Antol et al., 2015; Suhr et al., 2017, 2019b), and commonsense reasoning (Talmor et al., 2019; Sap et al., 2019b). Even though it is such a fundamental tool, crowdsourcing use is largely guided by common practices and the personal experience of researchers. Developing a theory of crowdsourcing use for practical language problems remains an open challenge. However, there are various principles and practices that have proven effective in generating high quality and diverse data. This tutorial exposes NLP researchers to such data collection crowdsourcing methods and principles through a detailed discussion of a diverse set of case studies.

The selection of case studies focuses on challenging settings where crowdworkers are asked to write original text or otherwise perform relatively unconstrained work. Through these case studies, we discuss in detail processes that were carefully designed to achieve data with specific properties, for example to require logical inference, grounded reasoning or conversational understanding. Each case study focuses on data collection crowdsourcing protocol details that often receive limited attention in research presentations, for example in conferences, but are critical for research success. We introduce the task of each case study, and do not assume prior knowledge. Where possible, we highlight common trends, or otherwise key differences between the discussed case studies.

**Relevance to the NLP Community** Crowdsourcing techniques are commonly used, but rarely discussed in detail. This tutorial provides a detailed description of crowdsourcing decisions in complex scenarios and the reasoning behind them. NLP researchers aiming to develop new datasets, tasks and data collection protocols will find the content directly applicable to their own work. A strong understanding of data collection practices and the range of decisions they include will also aid researchers using existing dataset to critically assess the data they use, including its limitations.

**Post-tutorial Materials** The tutorial videos, slides and other material will be made available publicly online following the tutorial.

## 2 Structure and Content Overview

The tutorial spans three hours (180 minutes), and is divided into eight sections:

**Introduction (10 min)** A brief introduction to the tutorial structure, its goals, and the case studies.



*Proceedings of the 2021 Conference on Empirical Methods in Natural Language Processing: Tutorial Abstracts*, pages 1–6
Punta Cana and Online, November 10–11, 2021. 

**Background (20 min)** A high-speed recap of established crowdsourcing concepts and terms. We refer back to the content of this section in the case studies. This section includes the basic structure of a Mechanical Turk task (HIT), typical incentive mechanisms, typical communication mechanisms, typical worker qualification and screening mechanisms, as well as relevant results about the demographics and expressed preferences of crowdworkers and the crowdworker community.

**Case Study I: MultiNLI (45 min)** We discuss the MultiNLI (Williams et al., 2018) corpus, with primary focus on experiments from subsequent papers that extend or evaluate the data collection protocol used to create this dataset. MultiNLI is built around the task of natural language inference (a.k.a. textual entailment; Dagan et al., 2006; MacCartney, 2009): given two sentences, the task is to identify (roughly) whether the first sentence entails the second. We start with this case study not because of any unique success of the data collection protocol, but because MultiNLI and the natural language inference task have emerged as a popular testbed for data collection methods and for relevant data analysis methods in NLP. Topics include:

- The development of a simple crowdworker-writing protocol for natural language inference data (Marelli et al., 2014; Bowman et al., 2015; Williams et al., 2018)
- Known issues with artifacts, social bias, and debatable judgments in data collected under this protocol (Rudinger et al., 2017; Tsuchiya, 2018; Gururangan et al., 2018; Poliak et al., 2018; Pavlick and Kwiatkowski, 2019)
- Experiments evaluating data collection feasibility under variants of the base task definition (Chen et al., 2020; Bowman et al., 2020)
- Studies evaluating the feasibility of collecting data for the same task using alternative protocols (Nie et al., 2020; Kaushik et al., 2019; Bowman et al., 2020; Vania et al., 2020; Parrish et al., 2021)

**Case Study II: NLVR (25 min)** Natural Language for Visual Reasoning comprises two datasets, NLVR (Suhr et al., 2017) and NLVR2 (Suhr et al., 2019b), both study natural language sentences grounded in visual context.[1] The task is to determine whether a caption is true or false about a paired image. The data was collected to require reasoning about object quantities, comparisons between object properties, and spatial relations between objects. NLVR2 is used as evaluation data for numerous language-and-vision systems (e.g., Tan and Bansal, 2019; Chen et al., 2019c). Both datasets were crowdsourced with a contrastive captioning designed to elicit linguistically complex sentences and to naturally balance the datasets between true and false examples. NLVR2 also uses a tiered system during crowdsourcing including distinct pools of annotation tasks for experienced workers and new workers.

**Case Study III: CerealBar (25 min)** CerealBar (Suhr et al., 2019a) is a game designed for studying collaborative natural language interactions, released alongside a dataset of interactions between human players.[2] CerealBar emphasizes collaboration through natural language instruction between agents with differing abilities. Each of the agents can be a human user or a learned model. CerealBar has been used to design and train systems that follow instructions by grounding them in the surrounding environment and acting in the environment. The game rules were explicitly designed with the intent of eliciting rich collaborative interactions across many instructions, for example by allowing a pair of players that is scoring well to continue playing for longer, thereby collecting more data from successful collaborations. The CerealBar data collection process included a development of a community of players, which has demonstrated behavioral and linguistic change over the crowdsourcing process.

**Case Study IV: QuAC (25 min)** Question Answering in Context is a dataset for studying information seeking dialogs between a student and a teacher (Choi et al., 2018). Given a subject heading, a student questions a teacher, who responds by copying spans from a Wikipedia article. The goal of the pair is to maintain a dialog of sufficient length without encountering too many unanswerable questions. The task is to play the role of the teacher: answering questions of an interested student. The collection protocol is unique in that two unreliable workers had to be coordinated for sufficient time to accomplish a meaningful dialog. QuAC collection relied on several strategies to keep

[1] `http://lil.nlp.cornell.edu/nlvr/`

[2] `http://lil.nlp.cornell.edu/cerealbar/`

partners from leaving interactions, such as allowing workers to simultaneously participate in multiple related dialogs, a feedback system teachers used to help students formulate questions, and scaling incentives that included punitive elements.

**Case Study V: SOCIALIQA (25 min)** SOCIALIQA (Sap et al., 2019b) is the first large-scale benchmark to test model emotional and social reasoning through 38k questions about everyday situations. The distributional nature of social commonsense knowledge requires the answer candidates to cover the plausible and likely, as well as the plausible but unlikely, as opposed to right/wrong answer candidates as common in other QA benchmarks. SOCIALIQA introduces a question-switching technique for crowdsourcing these unlikely answers, to overcome the possible stylistic artefacts in negative answers (e.g., negations, out-of-context responses; Schwartz et al., 2017). Additionally, to achieve large-scale and broad coverage, SOCIALIQA used a multi-stage crowdsourcing pipeline to expand seed events from the ATOMIC (Sap et al., 2019a) commonsense knowledge graph into full-fledged social situations.

**Summary (5 min)** A brief summary of the tutorial, including the main takeaways from the different cases studies and repeating themes.

## 3 Breadth

The set of case studies covers a broad and diverse set of task types, including large-scale inference tasks (e.g., NLI), small-scale interactive tasks (e.g., CerealBar), and multi-modal grounded tasks (e.g., NLVR). The aim of this broad distribution is to cover the most common task and data scenarios in NLP. We focus on details that are rarely discussed fully in papers. The set of case studies covers a broad and diverse set of task types, including large-scale inference tasks (e.g., NLI), small-scale interactive tasks (e.g., CerealBar), and multi-modal grounded tasks (e.g., NLVR). The aim of this broad distribution is to cover the most common task and data scenarios in NLP. The case studies cover the research of four distinct research labs. For each case study, we will also discuss related work from other authors as is relevant. For example, the MultiNLI case study will include extensive discussion of followup work and the SocialIQA case study will discuss related commonsense resources. In addition, we will discuss relevant existing work to provide all necessary background (e.g., Dumitrache et al., 2018; Chen et al., 2019b; Ramírez et al., 2019).

## 4 Prerequistites

Broad familiarity with NLP tasks, empirical evaluation methods, and data collection practices. We introduce all the necessary terms and the specifics of each case study.

## 5 Reading List

We recommend reviewing the 2015 NAACL tutorial on crowdsourcing.[3] While we focus on unconstrained and complex case studies, the 2015 tutorial provides an overview of basic terms and methods that is a complementary background to our material. However, we review the required material in the background section, and do not assume a familiarity with the content of this prior tutorial. We also recommend reading the main papers describing each of the case studies (Williams et al., 2018; Suhr et al., 2017, 2019b,a; Choi et al., 2018; Sap et al., 2019b).

## 6 Presenters

**Alane Suhr**
PhD Student, Cornell University
suhr@cs.cornell.edu
https://alanesuhr.com
Alane's research focuses on grounded natural language understanding. Alane has designed crowdsourcing tasks for collecting language data to study situated natural language understanding. Alane co-presented a tutorial in ACL 2018.

**Clara Vania**
Applied Scientist, Amazon
vaniclar@amazon.co.uk
https://claravania.github.io/
Her research focuses on crowdsourcing, transfer learning, and multilingual NLU. Recently, she has been working on semi-automatic data collection for natural language inference and crowdsourcing methods for question answering.

**Nikita Nangia**
PhD student, New York University
nikitanangia@nyu.edu
https://woollysocks.github.io
Nikita's work focuses on crowdsourcing methods

[3] http://crowdsourcing-class.org/tutorial.html

and data creation for natural language understandingsoft. Her recent work explores using incentive structures to illicit creative examples. Nikita co-organized a tutorial on latent structure models for NLP at ACL 2019.

**Maarten Sap**
PhD student, University of Washington
msap@cs.washington.edu
http://maartensap.com/
His research focuses on endowing NLP systems with social intelligence and social commonsense, and understanding social inequality and bias in language. His substantial experience with crowdsourcing includes the collecting of the SOCIALIQA commonsense benchmark as well as the creation of knowledge graphs with inferential knowledge (ATOMIC, Social Bias Frames).

**Mark Yatskar**
Assistant Professor, University of Pennsylvania
myatskar@seas.upenn.edu
https://markyatskar.com/
His research focuses on the intersection of natural language processing and computer vision. Mark's work has resulted in the creation of datasets such as imSitu, QuAC and WinoBias and recent research has focused on gender bias in visual recognition and coreference resolution.

**Sam Bowman**
Assistant Professor, New York University
bowman@nyu.edu
https://cims.nyu.edu/~sbowman/
Sam works on data creation, benchmarking, and model analysis for NLU and computational linguistics. Sam has had a substantial role in several NLU datasets, including SNLI, MNLI, XNLI, CoLA, and BLiMP, and his recent work has focused on experimentally evaluating methods for crowdsourced corpus construction.

**Yoav Artzi**
Associate Professor, Cornell University
yoav@cs.cornell.edu
https://yoavartzi.com/
Yoav's research focuses on learning expressive models for natural language understanding, most recently in situated interactive scenarios. Yoav led tutorials on semantic parsing in ACL 2013, EMNLP 2014 and AAAI 2015.

## References

Stanislaw Antol, Aishwarya Agrawal, Jiasen Lu, Margaret Mitchell, Dhruv Batra, C. Lawrence Zitnick, and Devi Parikh. 2015. VQA: Visual question answering. In *IEEE International Conference on Computer Vision*, pages 2425–2433.

Yonatan Bisk, Deniz Yuret, and Daniel Marcu. 2016. Natural language communication with robots. In *Proceedings of the 2016 Conference of the North American Chapter of the Association for Computational Linguistics: Human Language Technologies.*

Samuel R. Bowman, Gabor Angeli, Christopher Potts, and Christopher D. Manning. 2015. A large annotated corpus for learning natural language inference. In *Proceedings of the 2015 Conference on Empirical Methods in Natural Language Processing*, pages 632–642, Lisbon, Portugal. Association for Computational Linguistics.

Samuel R Bowman, Jennimaria Palomaki, Livio Baldini Soares, and Emily Pitler. 2020. Collecting entailment data for pretraining: New protocols and negative results. In *Proceedings of EMNLP*.

Howard Chen, Alane Suhr, Dipendra Misra, Noah Snavely, and Yoav Artzi. 2019a. Touchdown: Natural language navigation and spatial reasoning in visual street environments. In *IEEE Conference on Computer Vision and Pattern Recognition.*

Quanze Chen, Jonathan Bragg, Lydia B. Chilton, and Dan S. Weld. 2019b. Cicero: Multi-turn, contextual argumentation for accurate crowdsourcing. In *Proceedings of the 2019 CHI Conference on Human Factors in Computing Systems*, CHI '19, page 1–14, New York, NY, USA. Association for Computing Machinery.

Tongfei Chen, Zhengping Jiang, Adam Poliak, Keisuke Sakaguchi, and Benjamin Van Durme. 2020. Uncertain natural language inference. In *Proceedings of the 58th Annual Meeting of the Association for Computational Linguistics*, pages 8772–8779, Online. Association for Computational Linguistics.

Yen-Chun Chen, Linjie Li, Licheng Yu, Ahmed El Kholy, Faisal Ahmed, Zhe Gan, Yu Cheng, and Jingjing Liu. 2019c. UNITER: Learning universal image-text representations. *ArXiv*, abs/1909.11740.

Eunsol Choi, He He, Mohit Iyyer, Mark Yatskar, Wen tau Yih, Yejin Choi, Percy Liang, and Luke Zettlemoyer. 2018. Quac: Question answering in context. In *Empirical Methods in Natural Language Processing.*

Ido Dagan, Oren Glickman, and Bernardo Magnini. 2006. The PASCAL recognising textual entailment challenge. In *Machine learning challenges. Evaluating predictive uncertainty, visual object classification, and recognising tectual entailment*, pages 177–190. Springer, New York, NY.

Anca Dumitrache, Oana Inel, Lora Aroyo, Benjamin Timmermans, and Chris Welty. 2018. Crowdtruth 2.0: Quality metrics for crowdsourcing with disagreement. In *Joint Proceedings SAD 2018 and CrowdBias 2018*, CEUR Workshop Proceedings, pages 11–18. CEUR-WS.

Suchin Gururangan, Swabha Swayamdipta, Omer Levy, Roy Schwartz, Samuel Bowman, and Noah A. Smith. 2018. Annotation artifacts in natural language inference data. In *Proceedings of the 2018 Conference of the North American Chapter of the Association for Computational Linguistics: Human Language Technologies, Volume 2 (Short Papers)*, pages 107–112. Association for Computational Linguistics.

Divyansh Kaushik, Eduard Hovy, and Zachary Lipton. 2019. Learning the difference that makes a difference with counterfactually-augmented data. In *International Conference on Learning Representations*.

Tushar Khot, Ashish Sabharwal, and Peter Clark. 2018. Scitail: A textual entailment dataset from science question answering.

Bill MacCartney. 2009. *Natural language inference*. Ph.D. thesis, Stanford University, Stanford, CA.

Marco Marelli, Stefano Menini, Marco Baroni, Luisa Bentivogli, Raffaella bernardi, and Roberto Zamparelli. 2014. A SICK cure for the evaluation of compositional distributional semantic models. In *Proceedings of the Ninth International Conference on Language Resources and Evaluation (LREC)*, pages 216–223, Reykjavik, Iceland. European Language Resources Association (ELRA).

Dipendra Misra, Andrew Bennett, Valts Blukis, Eyvind Niklasson, Max Shatkhin, and Yoav Artzi. 2018. Mapping instructions to actions in 3D environments with visual goal prediction. In *Proceedings of the Conference on Empirical Methods in Natural Language Processing*.

Yixin Nie, Adina Williams, Emily Dinan, Mohit Bansal, Jason Weston, and Douwe Kiela. 2020. Adversarial NLI: A new benchmark for natural language understanding. In *Proceedings of the 58th Annual Meeting of the Association for Computational Linguistics*, pages 4885–4901, Online. Association for Computational Linguistics.

Alicia Parrish, William Huang, Omar Agha, Soo-Hwan Lee, Nikita Nangia, Alex Warstadt, Karmanya Aggarwal, Emily Allaway, Tal Linzen, and Samuel R Bowman. 2021. Does putting a linguist in the loop improve nlu data collection? In *To appear in Findings of EMNLP*.

Ellie Pavlick and Tom Kwiatkowski. 2019. Inherent disagreements in human textual inferences. *Transactions of the Association for Computational Linguistics*, 7:677–694.

Adam Poliak, Jason Naradowsky, Aparajita Haldar, Rachel Rudinger, and Benjamin Van Durme. 2018. Hypothesis only baselines in natural language inference. In *Proceedings of the Seventh Joint Conference on Lexical and Computational Semantics*, pages 180–191, New Orleans, Louisiana. Association for Computational Linguistics.

Pranav Rajpurkar, Jian Zhang, Konstantin Lopyrev, and Percy Liang. 2016. SQuAD: 100,000+ questions for machine comprehension of text. In *Proceedings of the Conference on Empirical Methods in Natural Language Processing*.

Jorge Ramírez, Simone Degiacomi, Davide Zanella, Marcos Baez, Fabio Casati, and Boualem Benatallah. 2019. Crowdhub: Extending crowdsourcing platforms for the controlled evaluation of tasks designs. *arXiv preprint 1909.02800*.

Rachel Rudinger, Chandler May, and Benjamin Van Durme. 2017. Social bias in elicited natural language inferences. In *Proceedings of the First ACL Workshop on Ethics in Natural Language Processing*, pages 74–79, Valencia, Spain. Association for Computational Linguistics.

Maarten Sap, Ronan LeBras, Emily Allaway, Chandra Bhagavatula, Nicholas Lourie, Hannah Rashkin, Brendan Roof, Noah A Smith, and Yejin Choi. 2019a. Atomic: An atlas of machine commonsense for if-then reasoning. In *AAAI*.

Maarten Sap, Hannah Rashkin, Derek Chen, Ronan LeBras, and Yejin Choi. 2019b. Social iqa: Commonsense reasoning about social interactions. In *EMNLP*.

Roy Schwartz, Maarten Sap, Ioannis Konstas, Li Zilles, Yejin Choi, and Noah A Smith. 2017. The effect of different writing tasks on linguistic style: A case study of the roc story cloze task. In *CoNLL*.

Alane Suhr, Mike Lewis, James Yeh, and Yoav Artzi. 2017. A corpus of natural language for visual reasoning. In *Proceedings of the Annual Meeting of the Association for Computational Linguistics*.

Alane Suhr, Claudia Yan, Jack Schluger, Stanley Yu, Hadi Khader, Marwa Mouallem, Iris Zhang, and Yoav Artzi. 2019a. Executing instructions in situated collaborative interactions. In *Proceedings of the Conference on Empirical Methods in Natural Language Processing*.

Alane Suhr, Stephanie Zhou, Ally Zhang, Iris Zhang, Huajun Bai, and Yoav Artzi. 2019b. A corpus for reasoning about natural language grounded in photographs. In *Proceedings of the Annual Meeting of the Association for Computational Linguistics*.

Alon Talmor, Jonathan Herzig, Nicholas Lourie, and Jonathan Berant. 2019. CommonsenseQA: A question answering challenge targeting commonsense knowledge. In *Proceedings of the Conference of the*

*North American Chapter of the Association for Computational Linguistics: Human Language Technologies*.

Hao Tan and Mohit Bansal. 2019. LXMERT: Learning cross-modality encoder representations from transformers. In *Proceedings of the 2019 Conference on Empirical Methods in Natural Language Processing and the 9th International Joint Conference on Natural Language Processing (EMNLP-IJCNLP)*, pages 5100–5111, Hong Kong, China. Association for Computational Linguistics.

Masatoshi Tsuchiya. 2018. Performance impact caused by hidden bias of training data for recognizing textual entailment. In *Proceedings of the Eleventh International Conference on Language Resources and Evaluation (LREC 2018)*, Miyazaki, Japan. European Language Resources Association (ELRA).

Clara Vania, Ruijie Chen, and Samuel R. Bowman. 2020. Asking crowdworkers to write entailment examples: The best of bad options. In *Proceedings of AACL*.

Adina Williams, Nikita Nangia, and Samuel Bowman. 2018. A broad-coverage challenge corpus for sentence understanding through inference. In *Proceedings of the 2018 Conference of the North American Chapter of the Association for Computational Linguistics: Human Language Technologies, Volume 1 (Long Papers)*, pages 1112–1122. Association for Computational Linguistics.

# Financial Opinion Mining

**Chung-Chi Chen,** [1] **Hen-Hsen Huang,**[2,3] **Hsin-Hsi Chen**[1,3]
[1] Department of Computer Science and Information Engineering
National Taiwan University, Taiwan
[2] Institute of Information Science, Academia Sinica, Taiwan
[3] MOST Joint Research Center for AI Technology and All Vista Healthcare, Taiwan
cjchen@nlg.csie.ntu.edu.tw, hhhuang@iis.sinica.edu.tw
hhchen@ntu.edu.tw

## 1 Type and Length

We will provide a **three-hour introductory** tutorial, named Financial Opinion Mining.

## 2 Goal of the Tutorial

When it comes to financial opinion mining, bullish and bearish come into people's minds. However, more fine-grained information will be missed if we only focus on the market sentiment analysis of financial documents. Thanks to the recent "CS + X" trend, more interdisciplinary cooperation exists between computer science and other domains. In the "NLP + Finance" community, lots of recent works pay their attention to in-depth analysis of different kinds of financial documents rather than market sentiment prediction. For example, our previous works (Chen et al., 2018, 2019a) find that the numeral information extracted from financial social media data is comparable to the price targets extracted from professional analysts' reports. Keith and Stent (2019) analyze the pragmatic and semantic features in the earnings conference calls and discuss how these features influence the investor's decision-making process. Zong et al. (2020) point out the difference between the textual factors and cognitive factors by comparing the accurate and inaccurate professional analysts' reports. The above-mentioned works conclude the necessity of capturing fine-grained opinions in the financial narratives. As the increasing interest of our community on this topic, recently, more and more related workshops spring up in the leading conferences, including FinWeb-2021 in the Web Conference, FinNLP-2021 in IJCAI, FinIR-2020 in SIGIR, and FNP-2020 in COLING.

In this tutorial, we will show where we are and where we will be to those researchers interested in this topic. We divide this tutorial into three parts, including coarse-grained financial opinion mining, fine-grained financial opinion mining, and possible research directions. This tutorial starts by introducing the components in a financial opinion proposed in our research agenda (Chen et al., 2021b) and summarizes their related studies. We also highlight the task of mining customers' opinions toward financial services in the FinTech industry, and compare them with usual opinions. Several potential research questions will be addressed. The audiences of this tutorial will gain an overview of financial opinion mining and figure out their research directions.

## 3 Tutorial Outline

We will cover the following topics based on recent works published in representative conferences and workshops. Both technical details and the application scenarios will be introduced. The contrast of financial opinion mining with general opinion mining will also be discussed. The characteristics of different kinds of financial documents will be listed.

### 3.1 Coarse-grained Financial Opinion Mining

The topic of the first session gives the overview of financial opinion mining, including the investor's opinion and the customer's opinion. We start with sentiment analysis in the financial domain. The comparison between the general sentiment and the market sentiment will also be discussed (Loughran and McDonald, 2011; Chen et al., 2020b). The lexicons for the sentiment analysis (Bodnaruk et al., 2015; Li and Shah, 2017; Sedinkina et al., 2019) in financial documents and the applications of adopting sentiment analysis results (Bollen et al., 2011; Du et al., 2019; Lin et al., 2020) will be included. This session also covers the sentiment analysis of financial narratives from different resources, including formal documents such as financial statements



*Proceedings of the 2021 Conference on Empirical Methods in Natural Language Processing: Tutorial Abstracts*, pages 7–10
Punta Cana and Online, November 10–11, 2021. 

and professional analyst's reports and informal documents such as blogs and social media platforms. The overview of applications on stock movement prediction and volatility forecasting will also be presented.

### 3.2 Fine-grained Financial Opinion Mining

The second session will focus on the fine-grained financial opinion mining, which is the recent trend in this field and also the research interest of the presenters. This session will start by the discussion of the aspect analysis of financial narratives (Maia et al., 2018; Chen et al., 2019a). The numeral in the textual data (Naik et al., 2019; Wallace et al., 2019; Chen et al., 2018, 2019a, 2020c) and the numeracy of the neural network models (Spithourakis and Riedel, 2018; Chen et al., 2019b) attract lots of attentions recently. In the financial narrative, the proportion of numerals are higher than that of other domains' documents. Without numerals, more important information will be missed. Thus, we summarize the related works for understanding the numerals in financial documents and provide a systematic analysis on these studies. The linguistic features of different kinds of financial documents will also be discussed (Keith and Stent, 2019; Zong et al., 2020), which can provide insights for the future works on feature engineering. The results of cross-document inference and comparison are also included (Chen et al., 2018; Keith and Stent, 2019).

### 3.3 Possible Research Directions

In the last session, we will discuss four possible research directions for future works (Chen et al., 2020a), including (1) argument mining in finance, (2) opinion quality evaluation, (3) implicit influence inference, and (4) opinion tracking in time series. We will link the proposed directions with the latest progress of NLP. For example, when introducing the ideas of argument mining in finance, we will provide a brief overview of current development on argument mining (Cabrio and Villata, 2018; Lawrence and Reed, 2019), and further present some instances for discussing the relation between current works and the proposed directions in financial opinion mining (Chen et al., 2020c). When discussing opinion quality evaluation, we will cover the studies of online review quality evaluation (Eirinaki et al., 2012; Wei et al., 2016; Ocampo Diaz and Ng, 2018), and show the difference between dealing with online reviews and dealing with financial opinions.

The audience will be inspired by this tutorial and find an interesting research direction for their work. With the discussion on the possible research directions, many novel ideas will be figured out during this tutorial.

## 4 Recommended Small Reading List

We recommend the audiences to read the following papers, which will be discussed in the tutorial.

- For understanding the difference between general sentiment analysis and financial sentiment analysis: Loughran and McDonald (2011)
- For having the picture of the basic application scenario: Bollen et al. (2011)
- The importance of numerals in the financial documents: Chen et al. (2018)
- For capturing the idea and the intent of fine-grained opinion mining: Keith and Stent (2019)
- For conceiving the proposed research directions: Chen et al. (2021a)

## 5 Presenters

**Chung-Chi Chen**[1] is currently a postdoctoral researcher at the MOST Joint Research Center for AI Technology and All Vista Healthcare, Taiwan. He got the Ph.D. degree in the Department of Computer Science and Information Engineering at National Taiwan University. He received the M.S. degree in Quantitative Finance from National Tsing Hua University, Taiwan. His research focuses on opinion mining and sentiment analysis in finance. He is the organizer of FinNum shared task series in NTCIR (2018-2022) and the FinNLP workshop series in IJCAI (2019-2021). He is the presenter of the AACL-2020 "Natural Language Processing in Financial Technology Applications" tutorial and the presenter of the EMNLP-2021 "Financial Opinion Mining" tutorial. His work has been published in ACL, WWW, SIGIR, IJCAI, and CIKM, and served as PC members in ACL, AAAI, EMNLP, CIKM, and WSDM. He won the 1st prize in both the Jih Sun FinTech Hackathon (2019) and the Standard Chartered FinTech competition (2018), and the 2nd prize in both the Jih Sun FinTech

[1] `http://cjchen.nlpfin.com/`

Hackathon (2018) and the E.SUN FHC FinTech Hackathon (2017).

**Hen-Hsen Huang**[2] is an assistant research fellow at the Institue of Information Science, Academia Sinica, Taiwan. His research interests include natural language processing and information retrieval. His work has been published in ACL, SIGIR, WWW, IJCAI, CIKM, COLING, and so on. Dr. Huang received the Honorable Mention of Doctoral Dissertation Award of ACLCLP in 2014 and the Honorable Mention of Master Thesis Award of ACLCLP in 2008. He served as the registration chair of TAAI 2017, the publication chair of ROCLING 2020, and as PC members of representative conferences in computational linguistics including ACL, COLING, EMNLP, and NAACL. He was one of organizers of FinNum Task at NTCIR and FinNLP Workshop at IJCAI.

**Hsin-Hsi Chen**[3] received the Ph.D. degree in electrical engineering in 1988 from National Taiwan University, Taipei, Taiwan. Since August 2018, Hsin-Hsi Chen has been a distinguished professor in the Department of Computer Science and Information Engineering, National Taiwan University. He was conference chair of IJCNLP 2013, program co-chair of ACM SIGIR 2010, senior PC members of ACM SIGIR 2006, 2007, 2008 and 2009, area/track chairs of AAAI 2020, EMNLP 2018, ACL 2012, ACL-IJCNLP 2009 and ACM CIKM 2008, and PC members of many conferences (IJCAI, SIGIR, WSDM, ACL, COLING, EMNLP, NAACL, EACL, IJCNLP, WWW, and so on). He will be conference chair of ACM SIGIR 2023. He received Google research awards in 2007 and 2012, MOST Outstanding Research Award in 2017, and the AmTRAN Chair Professorship in 2018.

## References


Andriy Bodnaruk, Tim Loughran, and Bill McDonald. 2015. Using 10-k text to gauge financial constraints. *Journal of Financial and Quantitative Analysis*, pages 623–646.

Johan Bollen, Huina Mao, and Xiaojun Zeng. 2011. Twitter mood predicts the stock market. *Journal of computational science*, 2(1):1–8.

Elena Cabrio and Serena Villata. 2018. Five years of argument mining: a data-driven analysis. In *IJCAI*, pages 5427–5433.


[2]http://www.cs.nccu.edu.tw/~hhhuang/

[3]http://nlg.csie.ntu.edu.tw/advisor.php


Chung-Chi Chen, Hen-Hsen Huang, and Hsin-Hsi Chen. 2019a. Numeral attachment with auxiliary tasks. In *Proceedings of the 42nd International ACM SIGIR Conference on Research and Development in Information Retrieval*, pages 1161–1164.

Chung-Chi Chen, Hen-Hsen Huang, and Hsin-Hsi Chen. 2020a. Fine-grained opinion mining in financial data: A survey and research agenda. *arXiv preprint arXiv:2005.01897*.

Chung-Chi Chen, Hen-Hsen Huang, and Hsin-Hsi Chen. 2020b. Issues and perspectives from 10,000 annotated financial social media data. In *Proceedings of The 12th Language Resources and Evaluation Conference*, pages 6106–6110.

Chung-Chi Chen, Hen-Hsen Huang, and Hsin-Hsi Chen. 2020c. Numclaim: Investor's fine-grained claim detection. In *Proceedings of the 29th ACM International Conference on Information and Knowledge Management*.

Chung-Chi Chen, Hen-Hsen Huang, and Hsin-Hsi Chen. 2021a. *From Opinion Mining to Financial Argument Mining*. Springer Briefs in Computer Science.

Chung-Chi Chen, Hen-Hsen Huang, and Hsin-Hsi Chen. 2021b. A research agenda for financial opinion mining. In *Proceedings of the International AAAI Conference on Web and Social Media*, volume 15, pages 1059–1063.

Chung-Chi Chen, Hen-Hsen Huang, Yow-Ting Shiue, and Hsin-Hsi Chen. 2018. Numeral understanding in financial tweets for fine-grained crowd-based forecasting. In *2018 IEEE/WIC/ACM International Conference on Web Intelligence (WI)*, pages 136–143. IEEE.

Chung-Chi Chen, Hen-Hsen Huang, Hiroya Takamura, and Hsin-Hsi Chen. 2019b. Numeracy-600K: Learning numeracy for detecting exaggerated information in market comments. In *Proceedings of the 57th Annual Meeting of the Association for Computational Linguistics*, pages 6307–6313, Florence, Italy. Association for Computational Linguistics.

Chi-Han Du, Ming-Feng Tsai, and Chuan-Ju Wang. 2019. Beyond word-level to sentence-level sentiment analysis for financial reports. In *ICASSP 2019-2019 IEEE International Conference on Acoustics, Speech and Signal Processing (ICASSP)*, pages 1562–1566. IEEE.

Magdalini Eirinaki, Shamita Pisal, and Japinder Singh. 2012. Feature-based opinion mining and ranking. *Journal of Computer and System Sciences*, 78(4):1175–1184.

Katherine Keith and Amanda Stent. 2019. Modeling financial analysts' decision making via the pragmatics and semantics of earnings calls. In *Proceedings of the 57th Annual Meeting of the Association for Computational Linguistics*, pages 493–503, Florence, Italy. Association for Computational Linguistics.

John Lawrence and Chris Reed. 2019. Argument mining: A survey. *Computational Linguistics*, pages 1–54.

Quanzhi Li and Sameena Shah. 2017. Learning stock market sentiment lexicon and sentiment-oriented word vector from StockTwits. In *Proceedings of the 21st Conference on Computational Natural Language Learning (CoNLL 2017)*, pages 301–310, Vancouver, Canada. Association for Computational Linguistics.

Sheng-Chieh Lin, Wen-Yuh Su, Po-Chuan Chien, Ming-Feng Tsai, and Chuan-Ju Wang. 2020. Self-attentive sentimental sentence embedding for sentiment analysis. In *ICASSP 2020-2020 IEEE International Conference on Acoustics, Speech and Signal Processing (ICASSP)*, pages 1678–1682. IEEE.

Tim Loughran and Bill McDonald. 2011. When is a liability not a liability? textual analysis, dictionaries, and 10-ks. *The Journal of Finance*, 66(1):35–65.

Macedo Maia, Siegfried Handschuh, André Freitas, Brian Davis, Ross McDermott, Manel Zarrouk, and Alexandra Balahur. 2018. Www'18 open challenge: financial opinion mining and question answering. In *Companion Proceedings of the The Web Conference 2018*, pages 1941–1942.

Aakanksha Naik, Abhilasha Ravichander, Carolyn Rose, and Eduard Hovy. 2019. Exploring numeracy in word embeddings. In *Proceedings of the 57th Annual Meeting of the Association for Computational Linguistics*, pages 3374–3380, Florence, Italy. Association for Computational Linguistics.

Gerardo Ocampo Diaz and Vincent Ng. 2018. Modeling and prediction of online product review helpfulness: A survey. In *Proceedings of the 56th Annual Meeting of the Association for Computational Linguistics*, pages 698–708, Melbourne, Australia. Association for Computational Linguistics.

Marina Sedinkina, Nikolas Breitkopf, and Hinrich Schütze. 2019. Automatic domain adaptation outperforms manual domain adaptation for predicting financial outcomes. In *Proceedings of the 57th Annual Meeting of the Association for Computational Linguistics*, pages 346–359, Florence, Italy. Association for Computational Linguistics.

Georgios Spithourakis and Sebastian Riedel. 2018. Numeracy for language models: Evaluating and improving their ability to predict numbers. In *Proceedings of the 56th Annual Meeting of the Association for Computational Linguistics (Volume 1: Long Papers)*, pages 2104–2115, Melbourne, Australia. Association for Computational Linguistics.

Eric Wallace, Yizhong Wang, Sujian Li, Sameer Singh, and Matt Gardner. 2019. Do NLP models know numbers? probing numeracy in embeddings. In *Proceedings of the 2019 Conference on Empirical Methods in Natural Language Processing and the 9th International Joint Conference on Natural Language Processing (EMNLP-IJCNLP)*, pages 5307–5315, Hong Kong, China. Association for Computational Linguistics.

Zhongyu Wei, Yang Liu, and Yi Li. 2016. Is this post persuasive? ranking argumentative comments in online forum. In *Proceedings of the 54th Annual Meeting of the Association for Computational Linguistics*, pages 195–200, Berlin, Germany. Association for Computational Linguistics.

Shi Zong, Alan Ritter, and Eduard Hovy. 2020. Measuring forecasting skill from text. In *Proceedings of the 58th Annual Meeting of the Association for Computational Linguistics*, pages 5317–5331, Online. Association for Computational Linguistics.

# Knowledge-Enriched Natural Language Generation

**Wenhao Yu**[1], **Meng Jiang**[1], **Zhiting Hu**[2], **Qingyun Wang**[3], **Heng Ji**[3], **Nazneen Rajani**[4]
[1]University of Notre Dame, [2]University of California, San Diego,
[3]University of Illinois Urbana-Champaign, [4]Salesforce Research
{wyu1, mjiang2}@nd.edu, zhitinghu@gmail.com,
{qingyun4, hengji}@illinois.edu, nazneen.rajani@salesforce.com

## 1 Introduction

Natural Language Generation (NLG) aims at deliberately constructing a natural language text in order to meet specified communicative goals. NLG has been applied in many real-world applications, including dialogue systems, biography generation, technical paper draft generation, and multimedia news summarization. Neural language models have achieved impressive successes at automatic NLG, especially on creative writing such as story completion and poetry generation. However, in many downstream applications such as news summarization, counter-argument narrative generation, and knowledge base description, the generation process needs to be guided by certain level of knowledge such as sentiment (Hu et al., 2017), topic (Xing et al., 2017), and style (Tikhonov et al., 2019).

The usage of supportive knowledge in NLG can be roughly divided into the following two levels: (1) knowledge description (KD), which transforms structured data into unstructured text, such as topic-to-text (Dong et al., 2021; Yu et al., 2021), knowledge base description (Gardent et al., 2017; Liu et al., 2018a; Qin et al., 2019; Zeng et al., 2021), table-to-text generation (Liu et al., 2018b; Moryossef et al., 2019; Wang et al., 2020) and its variants in low-resource (Ma et al., 2019) and multi-lingual setting (Kaffee et al., 2018), data-to-text (Wiseman et al., 2017; Puduppully et al., 2019), and graph-to-text (Song et al., 2018; Zhu et al., 2019; Yao et al., 2020); (2) knowledge synthesis (KS), which obtain knowledge from external knowledge resources (e.g, knowledge base) and integrate it into text generation, such as image or video caption generation (Whitehead et al., 2018; Lu et al., 2018), knowledge graph-supported dialogue generation (Liu et al., 2019; Zhang et al., 2020), knowledge-guided comment generation (Li et al., 2019), and scientific paper generation (Wang et al., 2019; Koncel-Kedziorski et al., 2019).

Knowledge-enriched text generation poses unique challenges in modeling and learning, driving active research in several core directions, ranging from integrated modeling of neural representations and symbolic information in the sequential/hierarchical/graphical structures, learning without direct supervisions due to the cost of structured annotation, efficient optimization and inference with massive and global constraints, to language grounding on multiple modalities, and generative reasoning with implicit commonsense knowledge and background knowledge. In this tutorial we will present a roadmap to line up the state-of-the-art methods to tackle these challenges on this **cutting-edge** problem. We will dive deep into various technical components (as shown in Figure 1): how to represent knowledge, how to feed knowledge into a generation model, how to evaluate generation results, and what are the remaining challenges?

## 2 Brief Tutorial Outline

### 2.1 Motivation and Overview [20 mins]

At the beginning of the tutorial we will motivate the task of knowledge-driven NLG by showing a large variety of applications (e.g., KD and KS) in academia and industry which have been mentioned in the Introduction. We will present examples about the shortcomings of pure Seq2Seq or language models as well as the opportunities of using knowledge to enrich the generation. We categorize the input source knowledge and related advanced machine learning technologies in Figure 1. We will present the overview of this tutorial including language models (LMs) and knowledge representation, general learning and generation frameworks, a variety of NLG methods enriched by knowledge sources including semantics and structures, real-world applications, and discussions.



*Proceedings of the 2021 Conference on Empirical Methods in Natural Language Processing: Tutorial Abstracts*, pages 11–16
Punta Cana and Online, November 10–11, 2021. 

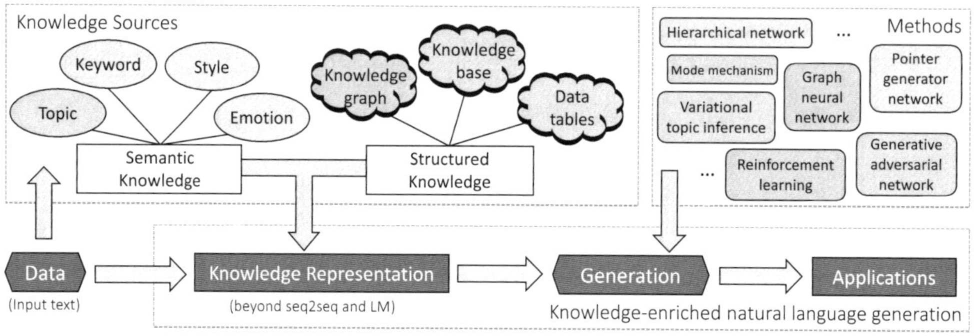


Figure 1: In this tutorial, we will present advanced NLG methods that inject knowledge from a variety of sources.

### 2.2 General Learning and Generation Frameworks [40 mins]

We will present the general methods of knowledge-enriched NLG, which provide the methodological foundations for incorporating different types of knowledge presented in the subsequent parts. Those methods are categorized into three major paradigms which incorporate knowledge through (1) *model architectures* that facilitate the use of knowledge, such as attention methods, copy/pointer mechanisms, graph neural networks (GNNs), knowledge-enriched embedding, etc; (2) *learning frameworks* that inject knowledge information into the generation models through training, such as posterior regularization, constraint-driven learning, semantic loss, knowledge-informed weak supervision, etc; (3) *inference methods* which imposes on the inference process different knowledge constraints to guide decoding, such as lexical constraints, task-specific objectives, global interdependency, etc.

### 2.3 NLG Methods Enhanced by Various Knowledge Sources: Part I [30 mins]

In this part, we present *semantic knowledge*-driven natural language generation. The semantic knowledge sources mainly contain keywords, topics, linguistic features, and other semantic constraints (e.g., style, emotion, sentiment). We introduce how the knowledge in each source can be encoded and how the represented knowledge can be decoded into natural language of high quality.

### 2.4 Coffee Break [30 mins]

### 2.5 NLG Methods Enhanced by Various Knowledge Sources: Part II [30 mins]

In this part, we present *structured knowledge*-driven natural language generation. The structured knowledge sources mainly contain tables, knowledge bases, and knowledge graphs. We introduce how the knowledge in each source can be represented and integrated into generation frameworks. Then, we introduce the methods that (i) find relevant knowledge (e.g., a relational path) from huge knowledge bases and knowledge graphs, and (ii) construct structured knowledge from text, e.g., OpenIE. Lastly, we introduce recent work that integrates multiple types of knowledge ranging from semantic, unstructured, to structured knowledge.

We will give a review of the available structured knowledge representation method, most of which focus on the structured tables. Traditionally, researchers tend to linearize the table for the input with the concatenation of type information. With computational advances in recent years, pre-trained language model based approaches for the linearized input have achieved significant success by combining type information as additional position embedding. However, those methods fail to consider the inter-dependency between different entities. We will discuss two major ways to learn those relations: self-attention mechanism and GNNs.

### 2.6 Applications [30 mins]

In this application session, we first review existing *potential applications* using the knowledge-driven generations. On one hand, the structured knowledge provides additional guidance for the major tasks such as dialogue systems, video captions , and summarizations. On the other hand, researchers have built independent knowledge guided generation tasks, starting from the data-to-text tasks such as Wikibio generation tasks in low-resource and multilingual setting, Webnlg contests, and ROTOWIRE, to more complex graph-to-text tasks such as AMR-to-text generation, scientific paper generation tasks, and news comment generation. Then, we will cover various post-processing approaches to enhance the quality of generation results for specific applciations, such as coverage mechanism, self-attention mechanism, and table-text optimal-transport matching loss. Finally we will briefly present how knowledge-enriched NLG is being used in several conversational AI systems including Amazon Alexa. Other commercial applications for NLG include systems that can retrieve and summarize information from a relational database into natural language text such as Salesforce's Einstein and Tableau.

### 2.7 Remaining Challenges and Future Directions [30 mins]

At the end of the tutorial we will discuss the remaining challenges and some of the future directions, including the challenge of capturing the inter-dependency of knowledge elements to make generated output coherent, knowledge reasoning, representing time and number, duplicate removal, augmenting massive pre-trained language models with external commonsense and background knowledge, and developing effective automatic evaluation metrics, and rigorous and efficient human evaluation procedures. We will provide pointers to resources, including data sets, software and on-line demos.

## 3 Diversity Considerations

The topic to be presented is of great interest to diverse group of audience from academics and industry. We will cover a broad diversity of methods and applications in many languages and domains. In particular, enriching modeling and learning with external knowledge, as the core topic in this tutorial, is particularly helpful for low-resource language modeling where no large data are available.

We have a diverse instructor team across multiple institutions (ND, UIUC, UCSD, and Salesforce Inc.) with varying seniority (ranging from junior/senior PhD students to assistant/full professors and senior researchers), two of whom are female researchers. The team has a diverse and broad expertise in natural language processing and generation, machine learning, data mining, and various application domains.

## 4 Prerequisites

This tutorial will present basic and advanced methods in NLG systematically to audience. The audience may find different useful content when have different levels of prior knowledge: (with the number of ☆ for how much a person may feel comfortable and confident with the subject matter)

- Familiar with Machine Learning from text, e.g., "Understand classification tasks and classical supervised methods on text data" (☆);
- Familiar with basic natural language processing (NLP) frameworks, e.g., "Had experience with LSTM, Seq2Seq, transformer" (☆☆);
- Familiar with some data forms of knowledge, e.g., "Had machine learning experience with topic modeling, knowledge bases, knowledge graphs, data tables, etc." (☆ ☆ ☆).

## 5 Reading List

Full reading list:
`https://github.com/wyu97/KENLG-Reading`
Small reading list:

- Survey: KENLG (Yu et al., 2020)
- General learning and NLG frameworks
  (1) Seq2Seq (Bahdanau et al., 2015),
  (2) Transformer (Vaswani et al., 2017),
  (3) Copy mechanism (Gu et al., 2016);
- Semantic knowledge for enhancing NLG
  (4) Topic (Xing et al., 2017),
  (5) Sentiment (Hu et al., 2017),
  (6) Emotion (Zhou et al., 2018a);
- Structured knowledge for enhancing NLG
  (7) Wikipedia KB (Liu et al., 2018b),
  (8) Sports Tables (Wiseman et al., 2017),
  (9) Commonsense KG (Zhou et al., 2018b),
  (10) Scientific KG (Koncel et al., 2019).

## 6 Presenters

**Wenhao Yu** is a Ph.D. student in the Department of Computer Science and Engineering at the University of Notre Dame. His research lies in controllable knowledge-driven natural language processing, particularly in natural language generation. His research has been published in top-ranked NLP and data mining conferences such as ACL, EMNLP, AAAI, WWW, and CIKM. Additional information is available at `https://wyu97.github.io/`

**Meng Jiang** is an assistant professor in the Department of Computer Science and Engineering at the University of Notre Dame. He received his B.E. and Ph.D. in Computer Science from Tsinghua University and was a postdoctoral research associate at the University of Illinois at Urbana-Champaign. His research interests focus on knowledge graph construction and natural language generation for news summarization and forum post generation. The awads he received include Notre Dame Faculty Award in 2019 and Best Paper Awards at ISDSA and KDD-DLG in 2020. Additional information is available at `http://www.meng-jiang.com/`.

**Zhiting Hu** is an assistant professor in Halıcıoğlu Data Science Institute at UC San Diego. He received his Ph.D. in Machine Learning from Carnegie Mellon University. His research interest lies in the broad area of natural language processing in particular controllable text generation, machine learning to enable training AI agents from all forms of experiences such as structured knowledge, ML systems and applications. His research was recognized with best demo nomination at ACL 2019 and outstanding paper award at ACL 2016. Additional information is available at `http://www.cs.cmu.edu/~zhitingh/`.

**Qingyun Wang** is a Ph.D. student in the Computer Science Department at the University of Illinois at Urbana-Champaign. His research lies in controllable knowledge-driven natural language generation, with a recent focus on the scientific paper generation. He served as a program committee in generation track for multiple conferences including ICML 2020, ACL 2019-2020, ICLR 2021, etc. He previously entered the finalist of the first Alexa Prize competition. Additional information is available at `https://eaglew.github.io/`

**Heng Ji** is a professor at Computer Science Department of University of Illinois at Urbana-Champaign, and Amazon Scholar. She has published on Multimedia Multilingual Information Extraction and Knowledge-enriched NLG including technical paper generation, knowledge base description, and knowledge-aware image and video caption generation. The awards she received include "Young Scientist" by World Economic Forum, "AI's 10 to Watch" Award by IEEE Intelligent Systems, NSF CAREER award, and ACL 2020 Best Demo Award. She has served as the Program Committee Co-Chair of many conferences including NAACL-HLT2018, and she is NAACL secretary 2020-2021. Additional information is available at `https://blender.cs.illinois.edu/hengji.html`.

**Nazneen Rajani** is a senior research scientist at Salesforce Research. She got her PhD in Computer Science from UT Austin in 2018. Several of her work has been published in ACL, EMNLP, NACCL, and IJCAI including work on generating explanations for commonsense and physical reasoning. Nazneen was one of the finalists for the VentureBeat Transform 2020 women in AI Research. Her work has been covered by several media outlets including Quanta Magazine, VentureBeat, SiliconAngle, ZDNet. More information on `https://www.nazneenrajani.com`

### 6.1 Selected Past Tutorials

**Heng Ji**:

- ACL'18 and CCL'18: Multi-lingual Entity Discovery and Linking
- SIGMOD'16: Automatic Entity Recognition and Typing in Massive Text Data.
- ACL'15: Successful Data Mining Methods for NLP.
- ACL'14 and NLPCC'14: Wikification and Beyond: The Challenges of Entity and Concept Grounding.
- COLING'12: Temporal Information Extraction and Shallow Temporal Reasoning.

**Meng Jiang**:

- KDD'20: Scientific Text Mining and Knowledge Graphs.
- KDD'20: Multi-modal Network Representation Learning: Methods and Applications.
- KDD'17: Mining Entity-Relation-Attribute Structures from Massive Text Data.
- KDD'17: Data-Driven Approaches towards Malicious Behavior Modeling.
- SIGMOD'17: Building Structured Databases of Factual Knowledge from Massive Text.
- WWW'17: Constructing Structured Information Networks from Massive Text Corpora.

**Zhiting Hu**:

- KDD'20: Learning from All Types of Experiences: A Unifying Machine Learning Perspective.
- AAAI'20: Modularizing Natural Language Processing.

## References

Dzmitry Bahdanau, Kyunghyun Cho, and Yoshua Bengio. 2015. Neural machine translation by jointly learning to align and translate. In *International Conference for Learning Representation (ICLR)*.

Xiangyu Dong, Wenhao Yu, Chenguang Zhu, and Meng Jiang. 2021. Injecting entity types into entity-guided text generation. In *Conference on Empirical Methods in Natural Language Processing (EMNLP)*.

Claire Gardent, Anastasia Shimorina, Shashi Narayan, and Laura Perez-Beltrachini. 2017. Creating training corpora for NLG micro-planners. In *Proceedings of the 55th Annual Meeting of the Association for Computational Linguistics (Volume 1: Long Papers)*, pages 179–188, Vancouver, Canada. Association for Computational Linguistics.

Jiatao Gu, Zhengdong Lu, Hang Li, and Victor O.K. Li. 2016. Incorporating copying mechanism in sequence-to-sequence learning. In *Proceedings of the 54th Annual Meeting of the Association for Computational Linguistics (Volume 1: Long Papers)*, pages 1631–1640, Berlin, Germany. Association for Computational Linguistics.

Zhiting Hu, Zichao Yang, Xiaodan Liang, Ruslan Salakhutdinov, and Eric P. Xing. 2017. Toward controlled generation of text. In *International Conference on Machine Learning (ICML)*.

Lucie-Aimée Kaffee, Hady Elsahar, Pavlos Vougiouklis, Christophe Gravier, Frédérique Laforest, Jonathon Hare, and Elena Simperl. 2018. Learning to generate Wikipedia summaries for underserved languages from Wikidata. In *Proceedings of the 2018 Conference of the North American Chapter of the Association for Computational Linguistics: Human Language Technologies, Volume 2 (Short Papers)*, pages 640–645, New Orleans, Louisiana. Association for Computational Linguistics.

Rik Koncel, Kedziorski, Dhanush Bekal, Yi Luan, Mirella Lapata, and Hannaneh Hajishirzi. 2019. Text generation from knowledge graphs with graph transformers. In *Conference of the North American Chapter of the Association for Computational Linguistics (NAACL-HLT)*.

Rik Koncel-Kedziorski, Dhanush Bekal, Yi Luan, Mirella Lapata, and Hannaneh Hajishirzi. 2019. Text Generation from Knowledge Graphs with Graph Transformers. In *Proceedings of the 2019 Conference of the North American Chapter of the Association for Computational Linguistics: Human Language Technologies, Volume 1 (Long and Short Papers)*, pages 2284–2293, Minneapolis, Minnesota. Association for Computational Linguistics.

Wei Li, Jingjing Xu, Yancheng He, ShengLi Yan, Yunfang Wu, and Xu Sun. 2019. Coherent comments generation for Chinese articles with a graph-to-sequence model. In *Proceedings of the 57th Annual Meeting of the Association for Computational Linguistics*, pages 4843–4852, Florence, Italy. Association for Computational Linguistics.

Shuman Liu, Hongshen Chen, Zhaochun Ren, Yang Feng, Qun Liu, and Dawei Yin. 2018a. Knowledge diffusion for neural dialogue generation. In *Proceedings of the 56th Annual Meeting of the Association for Computational Linguistics (Volume 1: Long Papers)*, pages 1489–1498, Melbourne, Australia. Association for Computational Linguistics.

Tianyu Liu, Kexiang Wang, Lei Sha, Baobao Chang, and Zhifang Sui. 2018b. Table-to-text generation by structure-aware seq2seq learning. In *AAAI Conference on Artificial Intelligence (AAAI)*.

Zhibin Liu, Zheng-Yu Niu, Hua Wu, and Haifeng Wang. 2019. Knowledge aware conversation generation with explainable reasoning over augmented graphs. In *Proceedings of the 2019 Conference on Empirical Methods in Natural Language Processing and the 9th International Joint Conference on Natural Language Processing (EMNLP-IJCNLP)*, pages 1782–1792, Hong Kong, China. Association for Computational Linguistics.

Di Lu, Spencer Whitehead, Lifu Huang, Heng Ji, and Shih-Fu Chang. 2018. Entity-aware image caption generation. In *Conference on Empirical Methods in Natural Language Processing (EMNLP)*.

Shuming Ma, Pengcheng Yang, Tianyu Liu, Peng Li, Jie Zhou, and Xu Sun. 2019. Key fact as pivot: A two-stage model for low resource table-to-text generation. In *Proceedings of the 57th Annual Meeting of the Association for Computational Linguistics*, pages 2047–2057, Florence, Italy. Association for Computational Linguistics.

Amit Moryossef, Yoav Goldberg, and Ido Dagan. 2019. Step-by-step: Separating planning from realization in neural data-to-text generation. In *Proceedings of the 2019 Conference of the North American Chapter of the Association for Computational Linguistics: Human Language Technologies, Volume 1 (Long and Short Papers)*, pages 2267–2277, Minneapolis, Minnesota. Association for Computational Linguistics.

Ratish Puduppully, Li Dong, and Mirella Lapata. 2019. Data-to-text generation with entity modeling. In *Proceedings of the 57th Annual Meeting of the Association for Computational Linguistics*, pages 2023–2035, Florence, Italy. Association for Computational Linguistics.

Libo Qin, Yijia Liu, Wanxiang Che, Haoyang Wen, Yangming Li, and Ting Liu. 2019. Entity-consistent end-to-end task-oriented dialogue system with KB retriever. In *Proceedings of the 2019 Conference on Empirical Methods in Natural Language Processing and the 9th International Joint Conference on Natural Language Processing (EMNLP-IJCNLP)*, pages 133–142, Hong Kong, China. Association for Computational Linguistics.

Linfeng Song, Yue Zhang, Zhiguo Wang, and Daniel Gildea. 2018. A graph-to-sequence model for AMR-to-text generation. In *Proceedings of the 56th Annual Meeting of the Association for Computational Linguistics (Volume 1: Long Papers)*, pages 1616–1626, Melbourne, Australia. Association for Computational Linguistics.

Alexey Tikhonov, Viacheslav Shibaev, Aleksander Nagaev, Aigul Nugmanova, and Ivan P. Yamshchikov. 2019. Style transfer for texts: Retrain, report errors, compare with rewrites. In *Proceedings of the 2019 Conference on Empirical Methods in Natural Language Processing and the 9th International Joint Conference on Natural Language Processing (EMNLP-IJCNLP)*, pages 3936–3945, Hong Kong, China. Association for Computational Linguistics.

Ashish Vaswani, Noam Shazeer, Niki Parmar, Jakob Uszkoreit, Llion Jones, Aidan N Gomez, Ł ukasz Kaiser, and Illia Polosukhin. 2017. Attention is all you need. In *Advances in Neural Information Processing Systems (Neruips)*. Curran Associates, Inc.

Qingyun Wang, Lifu Huang, Zhiying Jiang, Kevin Knight, Heng Ji, Mohit Bansal, and Yi Luan. 2019. PaperRobot: Incremental draft generation of scientific ideas. In *Proceedings of the 57th Annual Meeting of the Association for Computational Linguistics*, pages 1980–1991, Florence, Italy. Association for Computational Linguistics.

Zhenyi Wang, Xiaoyang Wang, Bang An, Dong Yu, and Changyou Chen. 2020. Towards faithful neural table-to-text generation with content-matching constraints. In *Proceedings of the 58th Annual Meeting of the Association for Computational Linguistics*, pages 1072–1086, Online. Association for Computational Linguistics.

Spencer Whitehead, Heng Ji, Mohit Bansal, Shih-Fu Chang, and Clare Voss. 2018. Incorporating background knowledge into video description generation. In *Proceedings of the 2018 Conference on Empirical Methods in Natural Language Processing*, pages 3992–4001, Brussels, Belgium. Association for Computational Linguistics.

Sam Wiseman, Stuart Shieber, and Alexander Rush. 2017. Challenges in data-to-document generation. In *Proceedings of the 2017 Conference on Empirical Methods in Natural Language Processing*, pages 2253–2263, Copenhagen, Denmark. Association for Computational Linguistics.

Chen Xing, Wei Wu, Yu Wu, Jie Liu, Yalou Huang, Ming Zhou, and Wei-Ying Ma. 2017. Topic aware neural response generation. In *AAAI Conference on Artificial Intelligence (AAAI)*.

Shaowei Yao, Tianming Wang, and Xiaojun Wan. 2020. Heterogeneous graph transformer for graph-to-sequence learning. In *Annual Meeting of the Association for Computational Linguistics (ACL)*.

Wenhao Yu, Chenguang Zhu, Zaitang Li, Zhiting Hu, Qingyun Wang, Heng Ji, and Meng Jiang. 2020. A survey of knowledge-enhanced text generation. *arXiv preprint arXiv:2010.04389*.

Wenhao Yu, Chenguang Zhu, Tong Zhao, Zhichun Guo, and Meng Jiang. 2021. Sentence-permuted paragraph generation. In *Conference on Empirical Methods in Natural Language Processing (EMNLP)*.

Qingkai Zeng, Jinfeng Lin, Wenhao Yu, Jane Cleland-Huang, and Meng Jiang. 2021. Enhancing taxonomy completion with concept generation via fusing relational representations. In *ACM SIGKDD International Conference on Knowledge Discovery & Data Mining (KDD)*.

Houyu Zhang, Zhenghao Liu, Chenyan Xiong, and Zhiyuan Liu. 2020. Grounded conversation generation as guided traverses in commonsense knowledge graphs. In *Proceedings of the 58th Annual Meeting of the Association for Computational Linguistics*, pages 2031–2043, Online. Association for Computational Linguistics.

Hao Zhou, Minlie Huang, Tianyang Zhang, Xiaoyan Zhu, and Bing Liu. 2018a. Emotional chatting machine: Emotional conversation generation with internal and external memory. In *AAAI Conference on Artificial Intelligence (AAAI)*.

Hao Zhou, Tom Young, Minlie Huang, Haizhou Zhao, Jingfang Xu, and Xiaoyan Zhu. 2018b. Commonsense knowledge aware conversation generation with graph attention. In *International Joint Conference on Artificial Intelligence (IJCAI)*.

Jie Zhu, Junhui Li, Muhua Zhu, Longhua Qian, Min Zhang, and Guodong Zhou. 2019. Modeling graph structure in transformer for better AMR-to-text generation. In *Proceedings of the 2019 Conference on Empirical Methods in Natural Language Processing and the 9th International Joint Conference on Natural Language Processing (EMNLP-IJCNLP)*, pages 5459–5468, Hong Kong, China. Association for Computational Linguistics.

# Multi-Domain Multilingual Question Answering

**Sebastian Ruder**
DeepMind
ruder@google.com

**Avirup Sil**
IBM Research AI
avi@us.ibm.com

## Abstract

Question answering (QA) is one of the most challenging and impactful tasks in natural language processing. Most research in QA, however, has focused on the open-domain or monolingual setting while most real-world applications deal with specific domains or languages. In this tutorial, we attempt to bridge this gap. Firstly, we introduce standard benchmarks in multi-domain and multilingual QA. In both scenarios, we discuss state-of-the-art approaches that achieve impressive performance, ranging from zero-shot transfer learning to out-of-the-box training with open-domain QA systems. Finally, we will present open research problems that this new research agenda poses such as multi-task learning, cross-lingual transfer learning, domain adaptation and training large scale pre-trained multilingual language models.[1]

## 1 Overall

Question answering (QA) has emerged as one of the most popular areas in natural language processing (NLP). Established benchmarks such as the Stanford Question Answering Dataset (SQuAD; Rajpurkar et al., 2016) are used as a standard testing ground for new models while open-domain QA benchmarks such as Natural Questions (Kwiatkowski et al., 2019) represent the frontier of what is possible with current NLP technology (Zaheer et al., 2020).

In this tutorial, we will review recent advances in open-domain QA but focus on an area that has received less attention both in research and in past tutorials—multi-domain and multilingual QA. Open-domain QA is of interest for building general-purpose assistants that can answer questions about any topic (Adiwardana et al., 2019). Most real-world applications of QA, however, deal with the needs of specific domains. Multi-domain QA is particularly promising as it allows us to adapt models to new domains that are of practical importance, such as answering questions about COVID-19 (Tang et al., 2020).

At the same time, over the course of the last year we have seen the emergence of the first benchmarks for multilingual QA (Lewis et al., 2020; Artetxe et al., 2020; Clark et al., 2020). These benchmarks are a step towards enabling access to technology beyond English and building question answering systems that serve all of the world's approximately 6,900 languages. In addition to introducing standard datasets for multilingual QA, we will discuss advances in cross-lingual learning that made such benchmarks viable for the first time.

We generally aim to highlight methods and techniques that can be applied to adapt to many domains and languages in order to be helpful to the majority of the audience. While multi-domain and multilingual data differ in many ways both can be formulated as transfer learning problems and approached using a similar set of fundamental tools and principles, which we aim to convey to our audience.

As one example of such a tool, we will cover training procedures for large pre-trained language models (LMs). For multi-domain QA, we will discuss adaptation of LMs *e.g.* BERT (Devlin et al., 2019) or RoBERTa (Liu et al., 2019). For multilingual QA, we will teach the methods for training LMs from large multilingual supervised and unsupervised data *e.g.* XLM-RoBERTa (Conneau et al., 2019) and M4 (Arivazhagan et al., 2019). Notably, our tutorial will highlight the challenges of applying such methods to specific domains and languages. Overall, we will aim to provide a set of best practices that will enable researchers and practitioners to train methods for their domain and

[1]The tutorial materials are available at https://github.com/sebastianruder/emnlp2021-multiqa-tutorial.



*Proceedings of the 2021 Conference on Empirical Methods in Natural Language Processing: Tutorial Abstracts*, pages 17–21
Punta Cana and Online, November 10–11, 2021. 

language of interest, from the nature of the training data, to model architectures and hyper-parameter settings.
**Type of the tutorial:** Cutting-edge.
**Prior QA tutorials at ACL:** The broader area of question answering has been a staple of tutorials at NLP conferences *e.g.* ACL 2018, ACL 2020. In general, we will demonstrate that techniques from open-domain QA cannot be directly applied to perform QA on unseen new domains (Tang et al., 2020; Castelli et al., 2020) and emphasize the importance of domain-specific training is necessary. This is the first tutorial to focus specifically on multi-domain and multilingual question answering, which has not been taught anywhere before.

**Breadth:** The tutorial will cover 90% of work from the QA, machine reading comprehension, domain adaptation and multilingual literature and 10% of the presenters work.
**Diversity:** The tutorial will cover multilingual work including discussions of large multilingual pre-trained language models and QA examples in different languages. We will also discuss how methods scale to different languages and domains, including how much training data is necessary to achieve a certain performance.
**Prerequisites:** Familiarity with Transformer models and pre-trained language models such as BERT.

## 2 Brief Tutorial Outline

This is a 3 hour tutorial: hence, we will divide our time between the following novel topics:

### 2.1 First half: Multi-Domain QA

1. **Open-Domain monolingual QA and its limitations [20 mins]:** We will begin our tutorial by introducing our audience to the existing work on open-domain QA (also known as reading comprehension) and its recent progress on benchmark tasks such as SQuAD (Rajpurkar et al., 2016, 2018) and Natural Questions (Kwiatkowski et al., 2019). We will then survey work on monolingual QA: giving a brief historical background, discussing the basic setup and core technical challenges of the research problem, and then describe modern datasets with the common evaluation metrics and benchmarks. Finally, we will discuss their limitations when applied to unseen closed domains e.g. movies, information technology (IT) or biomedical questions and motivate the next section.

2. **Introduce Multi-domain QA [20 mins]:** We will focus on several recent benchmark datasets *e.g.* TechQA (Castelli et al., 2020) and DoQA (Campos et al., 2020), which introduce more realistic QA scenarios. The former introduces a dataset and a leaderboard for IT that comes with only a limited amount of training data. The latter requires strong domain adaptation as QA systems are trained on the "cooking" domain and tested by answering questions about movies and travel. DoQA is rather challenging as QA systems need to take narrative context into consideration, which most reading comprehension systems do not. We will furthermore discuss recent datasets such as CovidQA (Tang et al., 2020), which focus on emerging domains that are of practical importance.

3. **Modeling and Evaluation [30 mins]:** Finally, we will focus on various initial baselines which can be adopted to achieve impressive results via transfer learning on top of large pre-trained language models such as BERT (Devlin et al., 2019). We will also discuss the evaluation methodology including the various metrics that measure document retrieval and QA performance. Finally, we give an overview of many practical ways to adapt to another domain such as via in-domain pretraining and *task-adaptive pretraining*, which improves performance by adapting to a task's unlabeled data (Gururangan et al., 2020).

### 2.2 Coffee Break: [30 mins]

### 2.3 Hour 2: Multilingual QA and open research problems

1. **From Mono to large Multilingual Language Models [15 mins]:** In this half we will first survey some of the large multilingual language models *e.g.* mBERT (Devlin et al., 2019), XLM (Conneau and Lample, 2019), XLM-R (Conneau et al., 2019), M4 (Arivazhagan et al., 2019). We will show how they have helped close the gap on cross-lingual tasks by introducing zero-shot cross-lingual learning.

2. **Multilingual QA [40 mins]:** Then we will give a comprehensive overview of several

non-English multilingual question answering datasets and systems such as DuReader (He et al., 2018) and DRCD (Shao et al., 2018) in Chinese, ARCD (Mozannar et al., 2019) in Arabic, multi-domain QA (Gupta et al., 2018) in Hindi-English, and visual QA (Gao et al., 2016) in Chinese-English. We distinguish between datasets that have been created by obtaining naturally occurring data in a language or via translations from SQuAD into Korean (Lee et al., 2018; Li et al., 2018), French and Japanese (Asai et al., 2018) and Italian (Croce et al., 2019). Recent datasets such as XQuAD (Artetxe et al., 2020) and MLQA (Lewis et al., 2020) cover more languages while the recently introduced TyDiQA (Clark et al., 2020) and MKQA (Longpre et al., 2020) can be seen as multilingual counterparts to Natural Questions. Three of these datasets are part of XTREME (Hu et al., 2020), a massively multilingual benchmark for testing the cross-lingual generalization ability of state-of-the-art methods. While state-of-the-art models have matched or surpassed human performance in general-purpose monolingual benchmarks such as GLUE (Wang et al., 2019), current methods still fall short of human performance on multilingual benchmarks, despite recent gains (Chi et al., 2020). Multilingual question answering consequently is at the frontier of such cross-lingual generalization. We will generally aim to highlight the settings where current methods fail, showing validation examples in different languages, and highlight best practices of how methods can be adapted to better deal with them.

3. **Open research problems [25 mins]:** Finally, we will discuss challenges and promising research directions for multi-domain and multilingual question answering.

## 3 Goals

### 3.1 What are the objectives of the tutorial?

Firstly, to familiarize the audience with the task of monolingual question answering and latest benchmarks on open-domain QA. We furthermore aim to raise awareness of the challenges of QA across multiple domains and languages, to demonstrate the usefulness of adapting models to such settings, and to teach best practices for different adaptation scenarios.

### 3.2 Why is this tutorial important to include at ACL?

Multi-domain and multilingual question answering is a key technology to deal with emerging topics and challenges around the world such as COVID-19 (Tang et al., 2020). We expect that being familiar and having access to the toolkit of multi-domain multilingual QA will both enable researchers to make progress on fundamental challenges and allow practitioners to leverage research advances in real-world applications. In addition, highlighting challenges and introducing the audience to techniques for adapting QA models to other languages may contribute to a broader, less English-centric research landscape.

## 4 Presenters

- **Name:** Sebastian Ruder
  **Affiliation:** DeepMind
  **Email:** `sebastian@ruder.io`
  **Website:** `http://ruder.io`
  Sebastian is a research scientist at DeepMind where he works on transfer learning and multilingual natural language processing. He has been area chair in machine learning and multilinguality for major NLP conferences including ACL and EMNLP and has published papers on multilingual question answering (Artetxe et al., 2020; Hu et al., 2020). He was the Co-Program Chair for EurNLP 2019 and has co-organized the 4th Workshop on Representation Learning for NLP at ACL 2019. He has taught tutorials on "Transfer learning in natural language processing" and "Unsupervised Cross-lingual Representation Learning" at NAACL 2019 and ACL 2019 respectively. He has also co-organized and taught at the NLP Session at the Deep Learning Indaba 2018 and 2019.

  **Section:** Sebastian will teach Multilingual QA during this tutorial (Second 1 1/2 hrs).

- **Name:** Avirup Sil
  **Affiliation:** IBM Research AI
  **Email:** `avi@us.ibm.com`
  **Website:** `http://ibm.biz/avirupsil`
  Avi is a Research Scientist and the Team Lead for Question Answering in the Multilingual NLP group at IBM Research AI. His team (comprising of research scientists and engineers) works on research on indus-

try scale NLP and Deep Learning algorithms. His team's system called 'GAAMA' has obtained the top scores in public benchmark datasets (Kwiatkowski et al., 2019) and has published several papers on question answering (Chakravarti et al., 2019; Castelli et al., 2020; Glass et al., 2020). He is also the Chair of the NLP professional community of IBM. Avi is a Senior Program Committe Member and the Area Chair in Question Answering for major NLP conferences *e.g.* ACL, EMNLP, NAACL and has published several papers on Question Answering. He has taught a tutorial at ACL 2018 on "Entity Discovery and Linking". He has also organized the workshop on the "Relevance of Linguistic Structure in Neural NLP" at ACL 2018. He is also the track coordinator for the Entity Discovery and Linking track at the Text Analysis Conference.

**Section:** Avi will teach Multi-domain QA during this tutorial (First 1 1/2 hrs).

## References


Daniel Adiwardana, Minh-thang Luong David, R So Jamie, Gaurav Nemade, Yifeng Lu, and Quoc V Le. 2019. Towards a Human-like Open-Domain Chatbot.

Naveen Arivazhagan, Ankur Bapna, Orhan Firat, Dmitry Lepikhin, Melvin Johnson, Maxim Krikun, Mia Xu Chen, Yuan Cao, George Foster, Colin Cherry, et al. 2019. Massively multilingual neural machine translation in the wild: Findings and challenges. *arXiv preprint arXiv:1907.05019*.

Mikel Artetxe, Sebastian Ruder, and Dani Yogatama. 2020. On the Cross-lingual Transferability of Monolingual Representations. In *Proceedings of ACL 2020*.

Akari Asai, Akiko Eriguchi, Kazuma Hashimoto, and Yoshimasa Tsuruoka. 2018. Multilingual extractive reading comprehension by runtime machine translation. *arXiv preprint arXiv:1809.03275*.

Jon Ander Campos, Arantxa Otegi, Aitor Soroa, Jan Deriu, Mark Cieliebak, and Eneko Agirre. 2020. DoQA–Accessing domain-specific FAQs via conversational QA. *ACL*.

Vittorio Castelli, Rishav Chakravarti, Saswati Dana, Anthony Ferritto, Radu Florian, Martin Franz, Dinesh Garg, Dinesh Khandelwal, Scott McCarley, Mike McCawley, et al. 2020. The TechQA Dataset. *Association for Computational Linguistics (ACL)*.

Rishav Chakravarti, Cezar Pendus, Andrzej Sakrajda, Anthony Ferritto, Lin Pan, Michael Glass, Vittorio Castelli, J William Murdock, Radu Florian, Salim Roukos, and Avirup Sil. 2019. CFO: A framework for building production nlp systems. *EMNLP-IJCNLP, Demo Track*.

Zewen Chi, Li Dong, Furu Wei, Nan Yang, Saksham Singhal, Wenhui Wang, Xia Song, Xian-Ling Mao, Heyan Huang, and Ming Zhou. 2020. InfoXLM: An Information-Theoretic Framework for Cross-Lingual Language Model Pre-Training. *arXiv preprint arXiv:2007.07834*.

Jonathan H. Clark, Eunsol Choi, Michael Collins, Dan Garrette, Tom Kwiatkowski, Vitaly Nikolaev, and Jennimaria Palomaki. 2020. TYDI QA: A Benchmark for Information-Seeking Question Answering in Typologically Diverse Languages. *Transactions of the ACL 2020*.

Alexis Conneau, Kartikay Khandelwal, Naman Goyal, Vishrav Chaudhary, Guillaume Wenzek, Francisco Guzmán, Edouard Grave, Myle Ott, Luke Zettlemoyer, and Veselin Stoyanov. 2019. Unsupervised cross-lingual representation learning at scale. *arXiv preprint arXiv:1911.02116*.

Alexis Conneau and Guillaume Lample. 2019. Cross-lingual language model pretraining. In *Advances in Neural Information Processing Systems*, pages 7057–7067.

Danilo Croce, Alexandra Zelenanska, and Roberto Basili. 2019. Enabling deep learning for large scale question answering in italian. *Intelligenza Artificiale*, 13(1):49–61.

Jacob Devlin, Ming-Wei Chang, Kenton Lee, and Kristina Toutanova. 2019. BERT: Pre-training of deep bidirectional transformers for language understanding. In *NAACL-HLT*.

Haoyuan Gao, Junhua Mao, Jie Zhou, Zhiheng Huang, Lei Wang, and Wei Xu. 2016. Multilingual image question answering. US Patent App. 15/137,179.

Michael Glass, Alfio Gliozzo, Rishav Chakravarti, Anthony Ferritto, Lin Pan, Bhargav GP Shrivatsa, Dinesh Garg, and Avirup Sil. 2020. Span selection pre-training for question answering. *Association for Computational Linguistics (ACL)*.

Deepak Gupta, Surabhi Kumari, Asif Ekbal, and Pushpak Bhattacharyya. 2018. Mmqa: A multi-domain multi-lingual question-answering framework for english and hindi. In *Proceedings of the Eleventh International Conference on Language Resources and Evaluation (LREC 2018)*.

Suchin Gururangan, Ana Marasović, Swabha Swayamdipta, Kyle Lo, Iz Beltagy, Doug Downey, and Noah A Smith. 2020. Don't stop pretraining: Adapt language models to domains and tasks. *ACL*.

Wei He, Kai Liu, Jing Liu, Yajuan Lyu, Shiqi Zhao, Xinyan Xiao, Yuan Liu, Yizhong Wang, Hua Wu, Qiaoqiao She, Xuan Liu, Tian Wu, and Haifeng Wang. 2018. DuReader: a Chinese machine reading comprehension dataset from real-world applications. In *Proceedings of the Workshop on Machine Reading for Question Answering*, pages 37–46, Melbourne, Australia. Association for Computational Linguistics.

Junjie Hu, Sebastian Ruder, Aditya Siddhant, Graham Neubig, Orhan Firat, and Melvin Johnson. 2020. Xtreme: A massively multilingual multi-task benchmark for evaluating cross-lingual generalization. *arXiv preprint arXiv:2003.11080*.

Tom Kwiatkowski, Jennimaria Palomaki, Olivia Redfield, Michael Collins, Ankur Parikh, Chris Alberti, Danielle Epstein, Illia Polosukhin, Matthew Kelcey, Jacob Devlin, Kenton Lee, Kristina N. Toutanova, Llion Jones, Ming-Wei Chang, Andrew Dai, Jakob Uszkoreit, Quoc Le, and Slav Petrov. 2019. Natural Questions: a benchmark for question answering research. *TACL*.

Kyungjae Lee, Kyoungho Yoon, Sunghyun Park, and Seung-won Hwang. 2018. Semi-supervised training data generation for multilingual question answering. In *Proceedings of the Eleventh International Conference on Language Resources and Evaluation (LREC 2018)*.

Patrick Lewis, Barlas Oğuz, Ruty Rinott, Sebastian Riedel, and Holger Schwenk. 2020. MLQA: Evaluating cross-lingual extractive question answering. *ACL*.

Jian Li, Zhaopeng Tu, Baosong Yang, Michael R Lyu, and Tong Zhang. 2018. Multi-head attention with disagreement regularization. In *EMNLP*, pages 2897–2903.

Yinhan Liu, Myle Ott, Naman Goyal, Jingfei Du, Mandar Joshi, Danqi Chen, Omer Levy, Mike Lewis, Luke Zettlemoyer, and Veselin Stoyanov. 2019. RoBERTa: A robustly optimized BERT pretraining approach. *CoRR*, abs/1907.11692.

Shayne Longpre, Yi Lu, and Joachim Daiber. 2020. MKQA: A Linguistically Diverse Benchmark for Multilingual Open Domain Question Answering. *arXiv preprint arXiv:2007.15207*.

Hussein Mozannar, Elie Maamary, Karl El Hajal, and Hazem Hajj. 2019. Neural Arabic question answering. In *Proceedings of the Fourth Arabic Natural Language Processing Workshop*, pages 108–118, Florence, Italy. Association for Computational Linguistics.

Pranav Rajpurkar, Robin Jia, and Percy Liang. 2018. Know what you don't know: Unanswerable questions for SQuAD. In *Proceedings of the 56th Annual Meeting of the Association for Computational Linguistics (Volume 2: Short Papers)*, pages 784–789, Melbourne, Australia. Association for Computational Linguistics.

Pranav Rajpurkar, Jian Zhang, Konstantin Lopyrev, and Percy Liang. 2016. SQuAD: 100,000+ questions for machine comprehension of text. *EMNLP*.

Chih Chieh Shao, Trois Liu, Yuting Lai, Yiying Tseng, and Sam Tsai. 2018. Drcd: a chinese machine reading comprehension dataset. *arXiv preprint arXiv:1806.00920*.

Raphael Tang, Rodrigo Nogueira, Edwin Zhang, Nikhil Gupta, Phuong Cam, Kyunghyun Cho, and Jimmy Lin. 2020. Rapidly Bootstrapping a Question Answering Dataset for COVID-19.

Alex Wang, Amanpreet Singh, Julian Michael, Felix Hill, Omer Levy, and Samuel R Bowman. 2019. GLUE: A Multi-Task Benchmark and Analysis Platform for Natural Language Understanding. In *Proceedings of ICLR 2019*.

Manzil Zaheer, Guru Guruganesh, Avinava Dubey, Joshua Ainslie, Chris Alberti, Santiago Ontanon, Philip Pham, Anirudh Ravula, Qifan Wang, Li Yang, and Amr Ahmed. 2020. Big Bird: Transformers for Longer Sequences. *arxiv preprint arxiv:2007.14062*, pages 1–51.

# Robustness and Adversarial Examples in Natural Language Processing

**Kai-Wei Chang**
University of California, Los Angeles
kwchang@cs.ucla.edu

**He He**
New York University
hehe@cs.nyu.edu

**Robin Jia**
Facebook AI Research and
University of Southern California
robinjia@fb.com

**Sameer Singh**
University of California, Irvine
sameer@uci.edu

## Abstract

Recent studies show that many NLP systems are sensitive and vulnerable to a small perturbation of inputs and do not generalize well across different datasets. This lack of robustness derails the use of NLP systems in real-world applications. This tutorial aims at bringing awareness of practical concerns about NLP robustness. It targets NLP researchers and practitioners who are interested in building reliable NLP systems. In particular, we will review recent studies on analyzing the weakness of NLP systems when facing adversarial inputs and data with a distribution shift. We will provide the audience with a holistic view of 1) how to use adversarial examples to examine the weakness of NLP models and facilitate debugging; 2) how to enhance the robustness of existing NLP models and defense against adversarial inputs; and 3) how the consideration of robustness affects the real-world NLP applications used in our daily lives. We will conclude the tutorial by outlining future research directions in this area.

**Type of Tutorial:** Cutting edge.

## 1 Tutorial Description

Recent advances in data-driven machine learning techniques such as deep neural networks have revolutionized natural language processing. In particular, modern natural language processing (NLP) systems have achieved outstanding performance on various tasks such as question answering, textual entailment, language generation. In many cases, they even achieve higher performance than inter-annotator agreement on benchmark datasets. It may be tempting to conclude from results on these *datasets* that current systems are as good as humans at these NLP *tasks*.

Despite the remarkable success, recent studies show that these systems often rely on spurious correlations and fail catastrophically when given inputs from different sources or inputs that have been adversarially perturbed. For example, Jia and Liang (2017) shows that state-of-the-art reading comprehension systems fail to answer questions about paragraphs that contain adversarially inserted sentences, which are automatically generated to distract computer systems without changing the correct answer. Similarly, a series of studies (e.g., (Ribeiro et al., 2018; Alzantot et al., 2018; Iyyer et al., 2018)) demonstrate that text classification models are not robust against adversarial examples that generated by synonym substitution, paraphrasing, and inserting/deleting characters in the text input. This lack of robustness exposes troubling gaps in current models' language understanding capabilities and creates problems when NLP systems are deployed to real users.

As NLP systems are increasingly integrated into people's daily lives and directly interact with end-users, it is essential to ensure their reliability. For example, systems that flag hateful social media content for review must be robust to adversaries who wish to evade detection (Hosseini et al., 2017). Defending against these threats requires building systems that are robust to whatever alterations an attacker might apply to text in order to achieve the desired classifier behavior. Besides, even if systems perform well on user queries on average, rare but catastrophic errors can lead to serious issues. In 2017, Facebook's machine translation system mistakenly translated an Arabic Facebook post with the message "Good morning" into a Hebrew phrase that meant "Attack them" (Berger, 2017). As a result, the Israeli police arrested the man who made the post and detained him for several hours until the misunderstanding is resolved. Therefore, deployed systems must avoid egregious errors like wrongly translating non-violent messages into violent ones and should be tested on "worst-case" non-violent



*Proceedings of the 2021 Conference on Empirical Methods in Natural Language Processing: Tutorial Abstracts*, pages 22–26
Punta Cana and Online, November 10–11, 2021. 

messages.

In this tutorial, we will review the history of adversarial example generation and methods for enhancing robustness of NLP systems. In particular, we will present recent community effort in the following topics:

- Algorithms for generating adversarial examples to "debug" NLP systems. We will cover a variety of approaches such as synonym substitution, syntactically controlled paraphrasing, character-level adversarial attacks and many applications, including sentiment analysis, textural entailment, question answering, and machine translation.
- Robustness to spurious correlations and methods for mitigating dataset bias.
- Adversarial data generation for collecting datasets.
- Certified robustness in NLP.
- Debugging and behavior testing of NLP models by adversarial and automatic data generation.
- Lessons and discussion on how to build reliable, accountable NLP systems.

The tutorial will bring researchers and practitioners to be aware of the robustness issues of NLP systems and encourage the research community to propose innovative solutions to develop robust, reliable, and accountable NLP systems.

## 2 Detail Outline

This tutorial presents a systematic overview of frontier approaches to generating adversarial examples to facilitate behavior testing and debugging of NLP systems. We will also review the studies revealing that NLP models make predictions based on spurious correlations learned in the data and discuss approaches to enhancing their robustness. We will motivate the discussion using various NLP tasks and will outline emerging research challenges on this topic at the end of the tutorial. The detailed contents covered in the tutorial are outlined below.

### Motivation

We will motivate the audience by demonstrating practical examples where NLP systems are brittle to adversarial examples and data distributional shifts. Then, we will outline the challenges of building reliable and robust NLP systems.

### Generating Adversarial Examples for Text Classification

Many NLP problems such as document categorization, sentiment analysis and textual entailment can be modeled as a text classification task. However, recent studies show that by slightly modifying a correctly classified example can cause the high-performing models to misclassify. We will discuss various algorithms for generating such adversarial examples and how these examples can be used to test the behaviors of models and facilitate debugging.

### Certified Robustness and Defending against Adversarial Attacks in NLP

Next, we will discuss methods for enhancing models against adversarial examples. Ensuring robustness to seemingly simple perturbations, such as typos or synonym replacements, is already challenging. In particular, since multiple parts of a sentence may be perturbed independently, there is a combinatorially large space of possible perturbations. We will discuss methods that augment training data with adversarial examples as well as methods that produce *certificates* of robustness. The latter enjoy computationally tractable guarantees that a model is correct on every allowed perturbation of a given input.

### Robustness to Spurious Correlations

Aside from adversarial attacks, current models are also prone to spurious correlations, i.e. predictive patterns that work well on a specific dataset but do not hold in general. As a result, models fail under a mild distribution shift. In this part, we will discuss methods that guard against known spurious correlations in the data and the robustness of large-scale pre-trained models.

### Adversarial data collection

Given the flaws in existing datasets, it seems likely that building robust NLP models will also require better ways to collect training data. In this part, we will discuss recent work that collects datasets using an adversarial data generation process, typically involving humans in the loop. We will also discuss connections with classical active learning approaches to data collection.

**Adversarial Trigger and Text Generation**

While most of the discussion in the tutorial focuses on natural language understanding, many language generation systems directly interact with end users and ensuring their robustness is equivalently important. In this part, we will discuss robustness issues in language generation tasks. We will also introduce adversarial triggers, input-agnostic sequences of tokens that trigger a model to produce a specific prediction when concatenated to any input from a dataset, and its application in conditional language generation.

**Conclusion, Future Directions, and Discussion**

We will conclude the tutorial by discussing future directions to promote robustness in NLP.

## 3 Reading List

While the tutorial will include our own work (Alzantot et al., 2018; Shi et al., 2019; Pezeshkpour et al., 2019; Ribeiro et al., 2020, 2018; Jia and Liang, 2017; Jia et al., 2019; Jones et al., 2020; He et al., 2019; Tu et al., 2020; Wallace et al., 2019a), we anticipate that roughly 60% of the tutorial content will pull from work by other researchers in NLP and machine learning communities, including (Huang et al., 2019; Ye et al., 2020; Nie et al., 2020; Wallace et al., 2019b; Pruthi et al., 2019; Zellers et al., 2018; Ren et al., 2019; Zhang et al., 2019; Belinkov et al., 2019; Chen et al., 2018; Zheng et al., 2020; Cheng et al., 2019; Hsieh et al., 2019; Abdou et al., 2020; Karimi Mahabadi et al., 2020; Karpukhin et al., 2019; Murray and Chiang, 2018; Iyyer et al., 2018; Ebrahimi et al., 2018). A more comprehensive list of related papers will be provided before the tutorial.

## 4 Prerequisite Knowledge

Our target audience is general NLP conference attendances; therefore, no specific knowledge is assumed of the audience except basic machine learning and NLP background:

- Understand derivatives and gradient decent methods as found in introductory Calculus.
- Understand the basic supervised learning paradigm and commonly used machine learning models such as logistic regression and deep neural networks.
- Familiar with common natural language processing concepts (e.g., parse trees, word representation) as found in an introductory NLP course.

## 5 Tutorial Instructors

Our instructors consist of experts who have conducted research in different aspects related to the tutorial topic.

**Kai-Wei Chang** Kai-Wei Chang is an assistant professor in the Department of Computer Science at the University of California Los Angeles. His research interests include designing robust, fair, and accountable machine learning methods for building reliable NLP systems (e.g., (Alzantot et al., 2018; Shi et al., 2019)). His awards include the EMNLP Best Long Paper Award (2017), the KDD Best Paper Award (2010), and the Sloan Resaerch Fellowship (2021). Kai-Wei has given tutorials at NAACL 15, AAAI 16, FAccT18, EMNLP 19, AAAI 20, MLSS 21 on different research topics. Additional information is available at `http://kwchang.net`.

**He He** He He is an assistant professor in the Department of Computer Science and the Center for Data Science at the New York University. Her research interests include reliable natural language generation and robust learning algorithms that avoid spurious correlations in the data (e.g., (He et al., 2019; Tu et al., 2020)). She has given tutorials at NAACL 15 and EMNLP 19. Additional information is available at `http://hhexiy.github.io`.

**Robin Jia** Robin Jia is currently a visiting researcher at Facebook AI Research, and will be an assistant professor in the Department of Computer Science at the University of Southern California starting in the Autumn of 2021. His research focuses on making natural language processing models robust to unexpected test-time distribution shifts (e.g., (Jia and Liang, 2017; Jia et al., 2019). Robin's work has received an Outstanding Paper Award at EMNLP 2017 and a Best Short Paper Award at ACL 2018. Additional information is available at `https://robinjia.github.io`.

**Sameer Singh** Sameer Singh is an Assistant Professor of Computer Science at the University of California, Irvine. He is working on large-scale and interpretable machine learning models for NLP (e.g., (Wallace et al., 2019a; Pezeshkpour et al., 2019)). His work has received paper awards at

ACL 2020, AKBC 2020, EMNLP 2019, ACL 2018, and KDD 2016. Sameer presented the Deep Adversarial Learning Tutorial (Wang et al., 2019) at NAACL 2019 and the Mining Knowledge Graphs from Text Tutorial at WSDM 2018 and AAAI 2017, along with tutorials on Interpretability and Explanations in upcoming NeurIPS 2020 and EMNLP 2020. Sameer has also received teaching awards at UCI. Website: `http://sameersingh.org/`

## References


Mostafa Abdou, Vinit Ravishankar, Maria Barrett, Yonatan Belinkov, Desmond Elliott, and Anders Søgaard. 2020. The sensitivity of language models and humans to Winograd schema perturbations. In *Proceedings of the 58th Annual Meeting of the Association for Computational Linguistics*.

Moustafa Alzantot, Yash Sharma, Ahmed Elgohary, Bo-Jhang Ho, Mani Srivastava, and Kai-Wei Chang. 2018. Generating natural language adversarial examples. In *Proceedings of the 2018 Conference on Empirical Methods in Natural Language Processing*.

Yonatan Belinkov, Adam Poliak, Stuart Shieber, Benjamin Van Durme, and Alexander Rush. 2019. On adversarial removal of hypothesis-only bias in natural language inference. In *Proceedings of the Eighth Joint Conference on Lexical and Computational Semantics (*SEM 2019)*.

Y. Berger. 2017. Israel arrests palestinian because facebook translated 'good morning' to 'attack them'. https://www.haaretz.com/israel-news/palestinian-arrested-over-mistranslated-good-morning-facebook-post-1.5459427.

Hongge Chen, Huan Zhang, Pin-Yu Chen, Jinfeng Yi, and Cho-Jui Hsieh. 2018. Attacking visual language grounding with adversarial examples: A case study on neural image captioning. In *Proceedings of the 56th Annual Meeting of the Association for Computational Linguistics (Volume 1: Long Papers)*.

Minhao Cheng, Wei Wei, and Cho-Jui Hsieh. 2019. Evaluating and enhancing the robustness of dialogue systems: A case study on a negotiation agent. In *Proceedings of the 2019 Conference of the North American Chapter of the Association for Computational Linguistics: Human Language Technologies, Volume 1 (Long and Short Papers)*.

Javid Ebrahimi, Daniel Lowd, and Dejing Dou. 2018. On adversarial examples for character-level neural machine translation. In *Proceedings of the 27th International Conference on Computational Linguistics*.

He He, Sheng Zha, and Haohan Wang. 2019. Unlearn dataset bias in natural language inference by fitting the residual. In *Proceedings of the 2nd Workshop on Deep Learning Approaches for Low-Resource NLP (DeepLo 2019)*.

H. Hosseini, S. Kannan, B. Zhang, and R. Poovendran. 2017. Deceiving Google's Perspective API built for detecting toxic comments. *arXiv preprint arXiv:1702.08138*.

Yu-Lun Hsieh, Minhao Cheng, Da-Cheng Juan, Wei Wei, Wen-Lian Hsu, and Cho-Jui Hsieh. 2019. On the robustness of self-attentive models. In *Proceedings of the 57th Annual Meeting of the Association for Computational Linguistics*.

Po-Sen Huang, Robert Stanforth, Johannes Welbl, Chris Dyer, Dani Yogatama, Sven Gowal, Krishnamurthy Dvijotham, and Pushmeet Kohli. 2019. Achieving verified robustness to symbol substitutions via interval bound propagation. In *Proceedings of the 2019 Conference on Empirical Methods in Natural Language Processing and the 9th International Joint Conference on Natural Language Processing (EMNLP-IJCNLP)*.

Mohit Iyyer, John Wieting, Kevin Gimpel, and Luke Zettlemoyer. 2018. Adversarial example generation with syntactically controlled paraphrase networks. In *Proceedings of the 2018 Conference of the North American Chapter of the Association for Computational Linguistics: Human Language Technologies, Volume 1 (Long Papers)*.

Robin Jia and Percy Liang. 2017. Adversarial examples for evaluating reading comprehension systems. In *Proceedings of the 2017 Conference on Empirical Methods in Natural Language Processing*.

Robin Jia, Aditi Raghunathan, Kerem Göksel, and Percy Liang. 2019. Certified robustness to adversarial word substitutions. In *Proceedings of the 2019 Conference on Empirical Methods in Natural Language Processing and the 9th International Joint Conference on Natural Language Processing (EMNLP-IJCNLP)*.

Erik Jones, Robin Jia, Aditi Raghunathan, and Percy Liang. 2020. Robust encodings: A framework for combating adversarial typos. In *Proceedings of the 58th Annual Meeting of the Association for Computational Linguistics*.

Rabeeh Karimi Mahabadi, Yonatan Belinkov, and James Henderson. 2020. End-to-end bias mitigation by modelling biases in corpora. In *Proceedings of the 58th Annual Meeting of the Association for Computational Linguistics*.

Vladimir Karpukhin, Omer Levy, Jacob Eisenstein, and Marjan Ghazvininejad. 2019. Training on synthetic noise improves robustness to natural noise in machine translation. In *Proceedings of the 5th Workshop on Noisy User-generated Text (W-NUT 2019)*.

Kenton Murray and David Chiang. 2018. Correcting length bias in neural machine translation. In *Proceedings of the Third Conference on Machine Translation: Research Papers*.

Yixin Nie, Adina Williams, Emily Dinan, Mohit Bansal, Jason Weston, and Douwe Kiela. 2020. Adversarial NLI: A new benchmark for natural language understanding. In *Proceedings of the 58th Annual Meeting of the Association for Computational Linguistics*.

Pouya Pezeshkpour, Yifan Tian, and Sameer Singh. 2019. Investigating robustness and interpretability of link prediction via adversarial modifications. In *Proceedings of the 2019 Conference of the North American Chapter of the Association for Computational Linguistics: Human Language Technologies, Volume 1 (Long and Short Papers)*.

Danish Pruthi, Bhuwan Dhingra, and Zachary C. Lipton. 2019. Combating adversarial misspellings with robust word recognition. In *Proceedings of the 57th Annual Meeting of the Association for Computational Linguistics*.

Shuhuai Ren, Yihe Deng, Kun He, and Wanxiang Che. 2019. Generating natural language adversarial examples through probability weighted word saliency. In *Proceedings of the 57th Annual Meeting of the Association for Computational Linguistics*.

Marco Tulio Ribeiro, Sameer Singh, and Carlos Guestrin. 2018. Semantically equivalent adversarial rules for debugging NLP models. In *Proceedings of the 56th Annual Meeting of the Association for Computational Linguistics (Volume 1: Long Papers)*.

Marco Tulio Ribeiro, Tongshuang Wu, Carlos Guestrin, and Sameer Singh. 2020. Beyond accuracy: Behavioral testing of NLP models with CheckList. In *Proceedings of the 58th Annual Meeting of the Association for Computational Linguistics*.

Zhouxing Shi, Huan Zhang, Kai-Wei Chang, Minlie Huang, and Cho-Jui Hsieh. 2019. Robustness verification for transformers. In *International Conference on Learning Representations*.

Lifu Tu, Garima Lalwani, Spandana Gella, and He He. 2020. An empirical study on robustness to spurious correlations using pre-trained language models. *TACL*.

Eric Wallace, Shi Feng, Nikhil Kandpal, Matt Gardner, and Sameer Singh. 2019a. Universal adversarial triggers for attacking and analyzing NLP. In *Proceedings of the 2019 Conference on Empirical Methods in Natural Language Processing and the 9th International Joint Conference on Natural Language Processing (EMNLP-IJCNLP)*.

Eric Wallace, Pedro Rodriguez, Shi Feng, Ikuya Yamada, and Jordan Boyd-Graber. 2019b. Trick me if you can: Human-in-the-loop generation of adversarial examples for question answering. *Transactions of the Association for Computational Linguistics*, 7.

Xiaozhi Wang, Xu Han, Zhiyuan Liu, Maosong Sun, and Peng Li. 2019. Adversarial training for weakly supervised event detection. In *Proceedings of the 2019 Conference of the North American Chapter of the Association for Computational Linguistics: Human Language Technologies, Volume 1 (Long and Short Papers)*.

Mao Ye, Chengyue Gong, and Qiang Liu. 2020. SAFER: A structure-free approach for certified robustness to adversarial word substitutions. In *Proceedings of the 58th Annual Meeting of the Association for Computational Linguistics*.

Rowan Zellers, Yonatan Bisk, Roy Schwartz, and Yejin Choi. 2018. SWAG: A large-scale adversarial dataset for grounded commonsense inference. In *Proceedings of the 2018 Conference on Empirical Methods in Natural Language Processing*.

Yeyao Zhang, Eleftheria Tsipidi, Sasha Schriber, Mubbasir Kapadia, Markus Gross, and Ashutosh Modi. 2019. Generating animations from screenplays. In *Proceedings of the Eighth Joint Conference on Lexical and Computational Semantics (*SEM 2019)*.

Xiaoqing Zheng, Jiehang Zeng, Yi Zhou, Cho-Jui Hsieh, Minhao Cheng, and Xuanjing Huang. 2020. Evaluating and enhancing the robustness of neural network-based dependency parsing models with adversarial examples. In *Proceedings of the 58th Annual Meeting of the Association for Computational Linguistics*.

# Syntax in End-to-End Natural Language Processing

**Hai Zhao[1], Rui Wang[1], and Kehai Chen[2]**
1 Department of Computer Science and Engineering,
Shanghai Jiao Tong University, Shanghai, China
2 Advanced Translation Technology Laboratory,
National Institute of Information and Communications Technology, Kyoto, Japan
zhaohai@cs.sjtu.edu.cn, wangrui.nlp@gmail.com, khchen@nict.go.jp

## Abstract

This tutorial surveys the latest technical progress of syntactic parsing and the role of syntax in end-to-end natural language processing (NLP) tasks, in which semantic role labeling (SRL) and machine translation (MT) are the representative NLP tasks that have always been beneficial from informative syntactic clues since a long time ago, though the advance from end-to-end deep learning models shows new results. In this tutorial, we will first introduce the background and the latest progress of syntactic parsing and SRL/NMT. Then, we will summarize the key evidence about the syntactic impacts over these two concerning tasks, and explore the behind reasons from both computational and linguistic background.

## 1 Tutorial Content

**Syntax** is the insightfulness about formal relative position inside languages, whose mathematical formalism was pioneered by Chomsky (1957). Syntactic parsing has been enduring for a significant progress since deep learning was fully introduced into natural language processing (NLP). We identify two development stages for parsing techniques by considering whether deep learning was involved or not. For the parsers that were built on traditional machine learning models, most work focus on designing better search algorithms or better structural modeling about syntax, while few ever consider feature engineering. For the parsers using deep learning models, most work turn to more effective and more salient representations, following the same structural formalization since the times of traditional parsers. We observe a series of significant performance improvement since 2014 (Chen and Manning, 2014; Dozat and Manning, 2017). In this part, we will survey the key language representation improvement for syntactic parsing. In general, syntactic information contributes to other end-to-end NLP tasks, such as SRL and MT. We summarize the contribution of syntax to SRL and MT in Table 1.

**Syntax in SRL**. SRL or semantic parsing as a computational job started since different semantic annotated datasets were released in recent two decades, which is trained by using PropBank such as Palmer et al. (2005). During treebank annotation, the semantic annotation may be naturally assigned onto syntactic constituents, so that it makes sense that the latter may help the former in either of linguistic explanation or machine learning procedure. Considering syntactic information helps or not, the performance variation of SRL may range about 5-10% in terms of traditional models. However, there has come new results since end-to-end SRL was proposed. Nearly all state-of-the-art SRL models, either span or dependency, have been based on LSTM backbone since Zhou and Xu (2015a). We attribute such a change of syntactic role to the effective distributional and contextualized representation offered by the LSTM from word embedding. Note that word embedding may have both syntactic and semantic sense.

Since the method by Zhou and Xu (2015b) and Marcheggiani et al. (2017), deep-learning-based SRL has obtained much less contribution from syntactic input. For either span or dependency SRL, deep models receive a less than 2% performance improvement even when perfect syntax (gold syntax labels) is introduced as shown by He et al. (2017a) and He et al. (2018a). We re-implemented the model of Li et al. (2019) and introduced a syntactic constraint in their span selection from a strong parser, which indicates that stronger syntax-agnostic models receive less enhancement from syntax information.



*Proceedings of the 2021 Conference on Empirical Methods in Natural Language Processing: Tutorial Abstracts*, pages 27–33
Punta Cana and Online, November 10–11, 2021. 

| Tasks | | Attention Mechanism | | | PreLM | Syntax | Effectiveness |
|---|---|---|---|---|---|---|---|
| | | attention | self-attention | biaffine | | | |
| Syntactic parsing | | | | ++ | ++ | | ++ |
| SRL | | | ++ | | | | ++ |
| | | | | ++ | ++ | + | ++ |
| NMT | RNN | ++ | | | 0 | + | ++ |
| | Self-attention | | ++ | | 0 | - | - |

Table 1: Role of different technical factors for the three NLP tasks. "++" denotes the significant performance contribution when used alone; "+" denotes the moderate contribution; "0" denotes mainly studies in zero/low-resource scenarios; "-" denotes negative or little impact. The mark in the rightmost column indicates whether it is overall effective when all marked factors to the left are combined.

**Syntax in MT** also endures a methodology change from statistical machine translation (SMT) (Brown et al., 1993) to neural machine translation (NMT) (Sutskever et al., 2014; Bahdanau et al., 2015) as the task of SRL. For typical SMT, besides phrase based SMT (Och et al., 1999; Koehn et al., 2003), syntactic (tree) based methods have been well developed (Yamada and Knight, 2001; Mi et al., 2008). In some scenarios, especially when the domain of the MT corpus is similar to the domain of the parsing corpus, the performance of tree based SMT is better than phrase based SMT (Koehn, 2009). For NMT, it so far achieves significant progress by using end-to-end based structure since 2014 (Sutskever et al., 2014; Bahdanau et al., 2015). Recently, self-attention based transformer (Vaswani et al., 2017) has become new state-of-the-art architecture in NMT and gives a series of new state-of-the-art benchmarks (Bojar et al., 2018; Marie et al., 2018; Wang et al., 2018a; Marie et al., 2019). Syntax information has been shown that it can improve the performances of the recurrent neural network (RNN) based NMT on conditions (Eriguchi et al., 2016, 2017; Chen et al., 2017a; Li et al., 2017; Wu et al., 2017; Chen et al., 2017b, 2018). However, so far it has not been shown significantly widely useful in self-attention based NMT. There are only a few work (Ma et al., 2019) adopted the syntactic information into the positional embedding of Transformer. We will give a detailed analysis on this issue by surveying the key technique details.

**Linguistic in MT**. In addition, we will investigate why linguistic cognition and prior knowledge can enhance the control of the dominant end-to-end neural framework, which makes the translation between a language pair proceed according to the expected and interpretable way. On one hand, linguistic cognition enables translation model (1) to reduce translation errors that violate common sense, such as over/under-translation questions (Tu et al., 2016), troublesome words modeling (Zhao et al., 2018b) and so on; (2) to have some basic abilities of human translator, for example, word importance modeling (Chen et al., 2020), translation refinement (Song et al., 2020), structured information (Xu et al., 2020), diverse feature (Chen et al., 2020) and so on. On the other hand, linguistic prior knowledge (i.e. alignment, bilingual lexicon, phrase table, and knowledge graphs) to alleviate the problem of inadequacy target translations which are caused by the language model property of the encoder-decoder framework (Feng et al., 2017; Zhang et al., 2017; Zhao et al., 2018a; Wang et al., 2018b). Moreover, linguistic differences between the source language and target language can learn natural language representations that are easy to be understood by the translation model, for example, word order difference (Chen et al., 2019; Ding et al., 2020), morphological differences (Ji et al., 2019) and so on. Meanwhile, linguistic shared feature between the source language and target language can also enhance the understanding and generation of natural language in MT, for example, shared words (Artetxe et al., 2018), image information (Yin et al., 2020), video information (Wang et al., 2020) and so on.

## 2 Relevance to the Computational Linguistics Community

The topics included in this tutorial, i.e., syntax parsing, SRL, and MT, are all the classic ones to the entire NLP/CL community. This tutorial is primarily towards researchers who have a basic understanding of deep learning based NLP. We believe that this tutorial would help the audience more deeply understand the relationship between three classic NLP tasks, i.e., syntax parsing and SRL/MT.

| Presenter: Hai Zhao | Presenter: Rui Wang and Kehai Chen | |
|---|---|---|
| 1. Syntactic Parsing (50 min) | 3. Syntax in MT (40 min) | 4. Summary (20 min) |
| 1.1 Traditional syntactic parsing | 3.1 Basics of MT | 4.1 Conclusion |
| 1.2 Neural syntactic parsing | 3.2 Syntax in RNN-based MT | 4.2 Future trends |
| 1.3 Basic of end-to-end NLP | 3.3 Syntax in self-attention based MT | |
| 2. Syntax in SRL (40 min) | 4.Linguistic in MT (30 min) | |
| 2.1 Basic of SRL | 4.1 Linguistic cognition for MT | |
| 2.2 Linguistic, Syntax, and Semantics | 4.2 Linguistic prior knowledge for MT | |
| 2.3 Syntax in end-to-end base SRL | | |
| Coffee Break (30 min) | | |

Table 2: Tutorial outlines

## 3 Type of the Tutorial: Cutting-edge

We introduce the cutting-edge technologies.

## 4 Tutorial Outlines

We will present our tutorial in three hours. The detailed tutorial outlines are shown in Table 1.

## 5 Breadth

20-30% of the tutorial covers work by the tutorial presenters and 70-80% by other researchers.

## 6 Diversity Considerations

N/A

## 7 Specification of Any Prerequisites for the Attendees

This tutorial is primarily aimed at researchers who have a basic understanding of NLP.

## 8 Small reading list

- Deep Learning: *Deep learning* (LeCun et al., 2015)
- Syntactic Parsing: *Deep biaffine attention for neural dependency parsing* (Dozat and Manning, 2016) and *Constituency parsing with a self-attentive encoder* (Kitaev and Klein, 2018).
- SRL: *Syntax for semantic role labeling, to be, or not to be* (He et al., 2018b) and *Deep semantic role labeling: What works and whats next* (He et al., 2017b).
- Machine Translation: *Statistical machine translation* (Koehn, 2009) and *Neural machine translation by jointly learning to align and translate* (Bahdanau et al., 2015).

## 9 Presenters

1. Dr. Hai Zhao, Professor, Department of Computer Science and Engineering, Shanghai Jiao Tong University, China.
`zhaohai@cs.sjtu.edu.cn`
`http://bcmi.sjtu.edu.cn/~zhaohai`

His research interest is natural language processing. He has published more than 120 papers in ACL, EMNLP, COLING, ICLR, AAAI, IJCAI, and IEEE TKDE/TASLP. He won the first places in several NLP shared tasks, such as CoNLL and SIGHAN Bakeoff and top ranking in remarkable machine reading comprehension task leaderboards such as SQuAD2.0 and RACE.

He has taught the course "natural language processing" in SJTU for more than 10 years. He is ACL-2017 area chair on parsing, and ACL-2018/2019 (senior) area chairs on morphology and word segmentation.

2. Dr. Rui Wang, Tenured Researcher, Advanced Translation Technology Laboratory, National Institute of Information and Communications Technology (NICT), Japan
`wangrui.nlp@gmail.com`
`https://wangruinlp.github.io`

His research focuses on machine translation (MT), a classic task in NLP. His recent interests are traditional linguistic based and cutting-edge machine learning based approaches for MT. He (as the first or the corresponding authors) has published more than 30 MT papers in top-tier NLP/ML/AI conferences and journals, such as ACL, EMNLP, ICLR, AAAI, IJCAI, IEEE/ACM transactions, etc. He has also won several first places in top-tier MT shared tasks, such as WMT-2018, WMT-2019, WMT-2020, etc.

He has given several tutorial and invited talks in

conferences, such as CWMT, CCL, etc. He served as the area chairs of ICLR-2021 and NAACL-2021.

3. Dr. Kehai Chen, Postdoctoral Researcher, Advanced Translation Technology Laboratory, National Institute of Information and Communications Technology (NICT), Japan
khchen@nict.go.jp
https://chenkehai.github.io

His research focuses on linguistic-motivated machine translation (MT), a classic NLP task in AI. He has published more than 20 MT and NLP papers in top-tier NLP/ML/AI conferences and journals, such as ACL, ICLR, AAAI, EMNLP, IEEE/ACM Transactions on Audio, Speech, and Language Processing, ACM Transactions on Asian and Low-Resource Language Information Processing, etc. He served as a senior program committee of AAAI-2021.

## 10 Previous Venues and Approximate Audience Sizes

There are some tutorials focusing on single NLP tasks, such as NMT in ACL-2016/IJCNLP-2018, semantic parsing in ACL-2018. In particular, the NMT tutorial at ACL-2016 (with around 800 registrations) had attracted around 150 attendees and the one at IJCNLP-2017 (with around 300 registrations) had attracted around 40 attendees.

Our tutorial will become the first one that explores the relationship between syntactic impact and end-to-end NLP tasks. As our topic is rather broader, we hope that this tutorial will attract around 100-200 attendees.

## 11 Special Requirements

None

## 12 Preferable Venue(s)

ACL-IJCNLP/EMNLP/NAACL-HLT/EACL

## 13 Open Access

Yes

## References

Mikel Artetxe, Gorka Labaka, Eneko Agirre, and Kyunghyun Cho. 2018. Unsupervised neural machine translation. In *International Conference on Learning Representations*.

Dzmitry Bahdanau, Kyunghyun Cho, and Yoshua Bengio. 2015. Neural machine translation by jointly learning to align and translate. In *International Conference on Learning Representations*, San Diego, CA.

Ondej Bojar, Rajen Chatterjee, Christian Federmann, Mark Fishel, Yvette Graham, Barry Haddow, Matthias Huck, Antonio Jimeno Yepes, Philipp Koehn, Christof Monz, Matteo Negri, Aurlie Nvol, Mariana Neves, Matt Post, Lucia Specia, Marco Turchi, and Karin Verspoor. 2018. Findings of the 2018 conference on machine translation (WMT18). In *Proceedings of the Third Conference on Machine Translation*, pages 272–307, Belgium, Brussels.

Peter F. Brown, Vincent J. Della Pietra, Stephen A. Della Pietra, and Robert L. Mercer. 1993. The mathematics of statistical machine translation: Parameter estimation. *Computational Linguistics*, 19(2):263–311.

Danqi Chen and Christopher D. Manning. 2014. A fast and accurate dependency parser using neural networks. In *Proceedings of EMNLP 2014*.

Huadong Chen, Shujian Huang, David Chiang, and Jiajun Chen. 2017a. Improved neural machine translation with a syntax-aware encoder and decoder. In *Proceedings of the 55th Annual Meeting of the Association for Computational Linguistics (Volume 1: Long Papers)*, pages 1936–1945, Vancouver, Canada.

K. Chen, R. Wang, M. Utiyama, E. Sumita, T. Zhao, M. Yang, and H. Zhao. 2020. Towards more diverse input representation for neural machine translation. *IEEE/ACM Transactions on Audio, Speech, and Language Processing*, 28:1586–1597.

Kehai Chen, Rui Wang, Masao Utiyama, Lemao Liu, Akihiro Tamura, Eiichiro Sumita, and Tiejun Zhao. 2017b. Neural machine translation with source dependency representation. In *Proceedings of the 2017 Conference on Empirical Methods in Natural Language Processing*, pages 2846–2852, Copenhagen, Denmark.

Kehai Chen, Rui Wang, Masao Utiyama, and Eiichiro Sumita. 2019. Neural machine translation with reordering embeddings. In *Proceedings of the 57th Annual Meeting of the Association for Computational Linguistics*, pages 1787–1799, Florence, Italy. Association for Computational Linguistics.

Kehai Chen, Rui Wang, Masao Utiyama, and Eiichiro Sumita. 2020. Content word aware neural machine translation. In *Proceedings of the 58th Annual Meeting of the Association for Computational Linguistics*, pages 358–364, Online. Association for Computational Linguistics.

Kehai Chen, Rui Wang, Masao Utiyama, Eiichiro Sumita, and Tiejun Zhao. 2018. Syntax-directed attention for neural machine translation. In *Proceedings of the AAAI Conference on Artificial Intelligence*, pages 4792–4799, New Olreans, LA.

Noam Chomsky. 1957. Syntactic structures. *Mouton*.

Liang Ding, Longyue Wang, and Dacheng Tao. 2020. Self-attention with cross-lingual position representation. In *Proceedings of the 58th Annual Meeting of the Association for Computational Linguistics*, pages 1679–1685, Online. Association for Computational Linguistics.

Timothy Dozat and Christopher D Manning. 2016. Deep biaffine attention for neural dependency parsing. *arXiv preprint arXiv:1611.01734*.

Timothy Dozat and Christopher D. Manning. 2017. Deep biaffine attention for neural dependency parsing. In *Proceedings of ICLR*.

Akiko Eriguchi, Kazuma Hashimoto, and Yoshimasa Tsuruoka. 2016. Tree-to-sequence attentional neural machine translation. In *Proceedings of the 54th Annual Meeting of the Association for Computational Linguistics (Volume 1: Long Papers)*, pages 823–833, Berlin, Germany.

Akiko Eriguchi, Yoshimasa Tsuruoka, and Kyunghyun Cho. 2017. Learning to parse and translate improves neural machine translation. In *Proceedings of the 55th Annual Meeting of the Association for Computational Linguistics (Volume 2: Short Papers)*, pages 72–78, Vancouver, Canada.

Yang Feng, Shiyue Zhang, Andi Zhang, Dong Wang, and Andrew Abel. 2017. Memory-augmented neural machine translation. In *Proceedings of the 2017 Conference on Empirical Methods in Natural Language Processing*, pages 1390–1399, Copenhagen, Denmark. Association for Computational Linguistics.

Luheng He, Kenton Lee, Mike Lewis, and Luke Zettlemoyer. 2017a. Deep semantic role labeling: What works and what's next. In *Proceedings of the 55th Annual Meeting of the Association for Computational Linguistics (Volume 1: Long Papers)*, pages 473–483, Vancouver, Canada.

Luheng He, Kenton Lee, Mike Lewis, and Luke Zettlemoyer. 2017b. Deep semantic role labeling: What works and what's next. In *Proceedings of the 55th Annual Meeting of the Association for Computational Linguistics (Volume 1: Long Papers)*, pages 473–483, Vancouver, Canada. Association for Computational Linguistics.

Shexia He, Zuchao Li, Hai Zhao, and Hongxiao Bai. 2018a. Syntax for semantic role labeling, to be, or not to be. In *Proceedings of the 56th Annual Meeting of the Association for Computational Linguistics (Volume 1: Long Papers)*, pages 2061–2071, Melbourne, Australia.

Shexia He, Zuchao Li, Hai Zhao, and Hongxiao Bai. 2018b. Syntax for semantic role labeling, to be, or not to be. In *Proceedings of the 56th Annual Meeting of the Association for Computational Linguistics (Volume 1: Long Papers)*, pages 2061–2071, Melbourne, Australia. Association for Computational Linguistics.

Yatu Ji, Hongxu Hou, Chen Junjie, and Nier Wu. 2019. Improving Mongolian-Chinese neural machine translation with morphological noise. In *Proceedings of the 57th Annual Meeting of the Association for Computational Linguistics: Student Research Workshop*, pages 123–129, Florence, Italy. Association for Computational Linguistics.

Nikita Kitaev and Dan Klein. 2018. Constituency parsing with a self-attentive encoder. In *Proceedings of the 56th Annual Meeting of the Association for Computational Linguistics (Volume 1: Long Papers)*, pages 2676–2686, Melbourne, Australia.

Philipp Koehn. 2009. *Statistical machine translation*. Cambridge University Press.

Philipp Koehn, Franz Josef Och, and Daniel Marcu. 2003. Statistical phrase-based translation. In *Proceedings of the 2003 Conference of the North American Chapter of the Association for Computational Linguistics on Human Language Technology - Volume 1*, pages 48–54, Edmonton, Canada.

Yann LeCun, Yoshua Bengio, and Geoffrey Hinton. 2015. Deep learning. *nature*, 521(7553):436.

Junhui Li, Deyi Xiong, Zhaopeng Tu, Muhua Zhu, Min Zhang, and Guodong Zhou. 2017. Modeling source syntax for neural machine translation. In *Proceedings of the 55th Annual Meeting of the Association for Computational Linguistics (Volume 1: Long Papers)*, pages 688–697, Vancouver, Canada.

Zuchao Li, Shexia He, Hai Zhao, Yiqing Zhang, Zhuosheng Zhang, Xi Zhou, and Xiang Zhou. 2019. Dependency or span, end-to-end uniform semantic role labeling. In *The Thirty-Third AAAI Conference on Artificial Intelligence*, Honolulu, Hawaii.

Chunpeng Ma, Akihiro Tamura, Masao Utiyama, Eiichiro Sumita, and Tiejun Zhao. 2019. Improving neural machine translation with neural syntactic distance. In *Proceedings of the 2019 Conference of the North American Chapter of the Association for Computational Linguistics: Human Language Technologies, Volume 1 (Long and Short Papers)*, pages 2032–2037, Minneapolis, Minnesota. Association for Computational Linguistics.

Diego Marcheggiani, Anton Frolov, and Ivan Titov. 2017. A simple and accurate syntax-agnostic neural model for dependency-based semantic role labeling. In *Proceedings of the 21st Conference on Computational Natural Language Learning (CoNLL 2017)*, pages 411–420, Vancouver, Canada.

Benjamin Marie, Haipeng Sun, Rui Wang, Kehai Chen, Atsushi Fujita, Masao Utiyama, and Eiichiro Sumita. 2019. NICT's unsupervised neural and statistical machine translation systems for the WMT19 news translation task. In *Proceedings of the Fourth Conference on Machine Translation (Volume 2: Shared Task Papers, Day 1)*, pages 294–301, Florence, Italy. Association for Computational Linguistics.

Benjamin Marie, Rui Wang, Atsushi Fujita, Masao Utiyama, and Eiichiro Sumita. 2018. NICT's neural and statistical machine translation systems for the WMT18 news translation task. In *Proceedings of the Third Conference on Machine Translation, Volume 2: Shared Task Papers*, pages 453–459, Brussels, Belgium.

Haitao Mi, Liang Huang, and Qun Liu. 2008. Forest-based translation. In *Proceedings of the 46th Annual Meeting of the Association for Computational Linguistics: Human Language Technologies*, pages 192–199, Columbus, Ohio.

Franz Josef Och, Christoph Tillmann, and Hermann Ney. 1999. Improved alignment models for statistical machine translation. In *Proceedings of the 1999 Joint SIGDAT Conference on Empirical Methods in Natural Language Processing and Very Large Corpora*, College Park, MD.

Martha Palmer, Daniel Gildea, and Paul Kingsbury. 2005. The proposition bank: An annotated corpus of semantic roles. *Computational Linguistics*, 31(1):71–106.

Kaitao Song, Xu Tan, and Jianfeng Lu. 2020. Neural machine translation with error correction. In *Proceedings of the Twenty-Ninth International Joint Conference on Artificial Intelligence, IJCAI-20*, pages 3891–3897. International Joint Conferences on Artificial Intelligence Organization. Main track.

Ilya Sutskever, Oriol Vinyals, and Quoc VV Le. 2014. Sequence to sequence learning with neural networks. In *Advances in Neural Information Processing Systems*, pages 3104–3112, Montral, Canada.

Zhaopeng Tu, Zhengdong Lu, Yang Liu, Xiaohua Liu, and Hang Li. 2016. Modeling coverage for neural machine translation. In *Proceedings of the 54th Annual Meeting of the Association for Computational Linguistics (Volume 1: Long Papers)*, pages 76–85, Berlin, Germany. Association for Computational Linguistics.

Ashish Vaswani, Noam Shazeer, Niki Parmar, Jakob Uszkoreit, Llion Jones, Aidan N. Gomez, Lukasz Kaiser, and Illia Polosukhin. 2017. Attention is all you need. *CoRR*, abs/1706.03762.

Rui Wang, Chenchen Ding, Masao Utiyama, and Eiichiro Sumita. 2018a. English-Myanmar NMT and SMT with pre-ordering: NICT's machine translation systems at WAT-2018. In *The 5th Workshop on Asian Translation*, Hong Kong, China.

X. Wang, Z. Tu, and M. Zhang. 2018b. Incorporating statistical machine translation word knowledge into neural machine translation. *IEEE/ACM Transactions on Audio, Speech, and Language Processing*, 26(12):2255–2266.

Xin Wang, Jesse Thomason, Ronghang Hu, Xinlei Chen, Peter Anderson, Qi Wu, Asli Celikyilmaz, Jason Baldridge, and William Yang Wang, editors. 2020. *Proceedings of the First Workshop on Advances in Language and Vision Research*. Association for Computational Linguistics, Online.

Shuangzhi Wu, Dongdong Zhang, Nan Yang, Mu Li, and Ming Zhou. 2017. Sequence-to-dependency neural machine translation. In *Proceedings of the 55th Annual Meeting of the Association for Computational Linguistics (Volume 1: Long Papers)*, pages 698–707, Vancouver, Canada.

Hongfei Xu, Josef van Genabith, Deyi Xiong, Qiuhui Liu, and Jingyi Zhang. 2020. Learning source phrase representations for neural machine translation. In *Proceedings of the 58th Annual Meeting of the Association for Computational Linguistics*, pages 386–396, Online. Association for Computational Linguistics.

Kenji Yamada and Kevin Knight. 2001. A syntax-based statistical translation model. In *Proceedings of the 39th Annual Meeting on Association for Computational Linguistics*, pages 523–530, Toulouse, France.

Yongjing Yin, Fandong Meng, Jinsong Su, Chulun Zhou, Zhengyuan Yang, Jie Zhou, and Jiebo Luo. 2020. A novel graph-based multi-modal fusion encoder for neural machine translation. In *Proceedings of the 58th Annual Meeting of the Association for Computational Linguistics*, pages 3025–3035, Online. Association for Computational Linguistics.

Jiacheng Zhang, Yang Liu, Huanbo Luan, Jingfang Xu, and Maosong Sun. 2017. Prior knowledge integration for neural machine translation using posterior regularization. In *Proceedings of the 55th Annual Meeting of the Association for Computational Linguistics (Volume 1: Long Papers)*, pages 1514–1523, Vancouver, Canada. Association for Computational Linguistics.

Yang Zhao, Yining Wang, Jiajun Zhang, and Chengqing Zong. 2018a. Phrase table as recommendation memory for neural machine translation. In *Proceedings of the 27th International Joint Conference on Artificial Intelligence*, IJCAI'18, page 46094615. AAAI Press.

Yang Zhao, Jiajun Zhang, Zhongjun He, Chengqing Zong, and Hua Wu. 2018b. Addressing troublesome words in neural machine translation. In *Proceedings of the 2018 Conference on Empirical Methods in Natural Language Processing*, pages 391–400, Brussels, Belgium. Association for Computational Linguistics.

Jie Zhou and Wei Xu. 2015a. End-to-end learning of semantic role labeling using recurrent neural networks. In *Proceedings of the 53rd Annual Meeting of the Association for Computational Linguistics and the 7th International Joint Conference on Natural Language Processing (Volume 1: Long Papers)*, pages 1127–1137, Beijing, China.

Jie Zhou and Wei Xu. 2015b. End-to-end learning of semantic role labeling using recurrent neural networks. In *Proceedings of the 53rd Annual Meeting of the Association for Computational Linguistics and the 7th International Joint Conference on Natural Language Processing (Volume 1: Long Papers)*, pages 1127–1137, Beijing, China.

# Author Index